FPL
204

Praise for
THE LITTLE BOOK ON MEANING

"Fortgang gives readers tools to find the deeper meaning in life that we're all looking for. Using her own experiences in life and as a coach, she shares her insights on how to reach the ease and flow that make for a peaceful and joyful existence."

—DR. LAURA BERMAN, author of the *New York Times* bestseller *Real Sex for Real Women*, and regular guest on *The Oprah Winfrey Show*

"*The Little Book on Meaning* is the grounded person's guide to shifting into a sweeter way of being. Laura Berman Fortgang shows us how, even with driven natures, depression, and worldly responsibilities, we can open up to the love and mysticism that provide the deliverance we crave. She is funny, real, and practical, and leaves you with a deep compassion for life."

—TAMA J. KIEVES, bestselling author of *This Time I Dance! Creating the Work You Love*

"Powerful, touching, insightful, and full of ways to unlock the wonder of living a life you love—*The Little Book on Meaning* is a treasure. Fortgang is a brilliant guide and a great companion in helping us find, and live from, what truly matters most."

—MARY MANIN MORRISSEY, author *Building Your Field of Dreams*

"In this wise book, Laura Berman Fortgang shares lovely stories from her own life and the lives of others to reveal how everyday people earn the hard-won wisdom that leads to the fulfillment of a meaningful life."

—JULIE MORGENSTERN, bestselling author of *Organizing from the Inside Out* and *Shed Your Stuff, Change Your Life*

"*The Little Book on Meaning* offers a spiritual philosophy and framework for life and can be shared with people of all faiths and ages. This book will touch every soul it crosses. A must read."

—GARY QUINN, bestselling author of *Living in the Spiritual Zone* and coauthor of *Angel Wisdom*

"*The Little Book on Meaning* is a search for more—the wise kind of 'more.' By giving the reader an honest and courageous glimpse into her own search for meaning, Laura Berman Fortgang has offered a gift that is sure to touch the heart of anyone who longs for a rich, soul-connected life."

—CHERYL RICHARDSON, *New York Times*–bestselling author of *Take Time for Your Life* and *The Art of Extreme Self-Care*

"This so-called little book packs a big punch. It is intelligent and lyrical, intimate and insightful, spiritual and earthy. And it reveals the meaning of true success and happiness."

—DR. ROBERT HOLDEN, author of *Happiness Now!* and director, Success Intelligence and The Happiness Project

"Fortgang goes to new depths in this book, and she brings us along with her. It can't help but raise your consciousness and allow you to recognize the meaning in all you do. What a blessing!"

—IYANLA VANZANT, author of *Tapping the Power Within*

"Fortgang speaks the truth. Her journey illuminates a path that, for so many, isn't easy or clear but is deeply desired. She lights the way for all of us. Read this book to find courage, reassurance, and peace."

—RHONDA BRITTEN, bestselling author of *Fearless Living,* and founder, Fearless Living Institute

"Meaning is one of those subjects I'm obsessed with. How do we make it, find it, feel it? Can we? Laura's personal, moving, honest, and funny exploration of our perennial yearning had me reading until late, dog-earing pages, and most of all, understanding meaning in a far deeper, truer way. What a nourishing exploration, one that will widen your ability to experience meaning every day and in the most heart-filling, satisfying way."

—JENNIFER LOUDEN, bestselling author of *The Woman's Comfort Book* and *The Life Organizer*

OTHER BOOKS BY LAURA BERMAN FORTGANG

Now What? 90 Days to a New Life Direction

Living Your Best Life:
Discover Your Life's Blueprint for Success

Take Yourself to the Top:
Success from the Inside Out

LAURA BERMAN FORTGANG

THE LITTLE BOOK ON MEANING

Why We Crave It, How We Create It

JEREMY P. TARCHER/PENGUIN

A MEMBER OF PENGUIN GROUP (USA) INC.

NEW YORK

JEREMY P. TARCHER/PENGUIN
Published by the Penguin Group
Penguin Group (USA) Inc., 375 Hudson Street, New York, New York 10014, USA •
Penguin Group (Canada), 90 Eglinton Avenue East, Suite 700, Toronto,
Ontario M4P 2Y3, Canada (a division of Pearson Canada Inc.) • Penguin Books
Ltd, 80 Strand, London WC2R 0RL, England • Penguin Ireland, 25 St Stephen's
Green, Dublin 2, Ireland (a division of Penguin Books Ltd) • Penguin Group
(Australia), 250 Camberwell Road, Camberwell, Victoria 3124, Australia (a division
of Pearson Australia Group Pty Ltd) • Penguin Books India Pvt Ltd, 11 Community
Centre, Panchsheel Park, New Delhi–110 017, India • Penguin Group (NZ),
67 Apollo Drive, Rosedale, North Shore 0632, New Zealand (a division of Pearson
New Zealand Ltd) • Penguin Books (South Africa) (Pty) Ltd, 24 Sturdee Avenue,
Rosebank, Johannesburg 2196, South Africa

Penguin Books Ltd, Registered Offices: 80 Strand,
London WC2R 0RL, England

Most Tarcher/Penguin books are available at special quantity discounts for bulk purchase
for sales promotions, premiums, fund-raising, and educational needs. Special books or book
excerpts also can be created to fit specific needs. For details, write Penguin Group (USA)
Inc. Special Markets, 375 Hudson Street, New York, NY 10014.

Library of Congress Cataloging-in-Publication Data

Fortgang, Laura Berman.
The little book on meaning : why we crave it, how we create it / Laura Berman Fortgang.
p.   cm
Includes bibliographical references and index.
ISBN 978-1-58542-715-4
1. Spirituality.   2. Meaning (Philosophy)—Religious aspects.   I. Title.
BL624.F6637   2009   2009005875
204—dc22

Printed in the United States of America
1   3   5   7   9   10   8   6   4   2

Book design by Jessica Shatan Heslin / Studio Shatan, Inc.

While the author has made every effort to provide accurate telephone numbers and Inter-
net addresses at the time of publication, neither the publisher nor the author assumes any
responsibility for errors, or for changes that occur after publication. Further, the publisher
does not have any control over and does not assume any responsibility for author or third-
party websites or their content.

TO MARK, SKYLER, MAYA, AND WYATT

You make it a meaningful life.

CONTENTS

What Is This Pain?

It starts as tightness in the upper solar plexus. Then it starts to droop like the top of an ice cream cone on a hundred-degree day, eventually melting over everything to form a vague coating of ambivalence. Sometimes it matures into hopelessness and, for some, even depression. The "it" is the yearning for meaning. And it can swallow you whole.

I started to feel it in my twenties as I struggled to cling to my dream of being a Broadway star while entering what would be my seventh year of waiting tables in New York City. I had given myself five years to make it, but by the seventh, I still needed to work "day jobs" to get by. It was at that point that, I remember, I first strained to hear some guidance about what I was meant to do with my life. The straining hurt, and the answers did not come quickly. Two years went by, my depression deepening into complete darkness, and then suddenly, meaning came for me in the form of painting floors and stuffing envelopes for the Manhattan Center for Living—a short-lived nonprofit organization that was a haven for people dealing with life-threatening illnesses. Doing menial work for a worthy cause gave more meaning to my life in a handful of Wednesday afternoons than all the years of slogging my way through college and a professional acting career did. It made more sense than the previous four years of therapy had too.

One day, as I painted the floor with white high-gloss paint, the rocking motion of rolling the roller and the sound of the paint separating from the roll and smacking on the floor, I was brought into a peaceful place. I felt comfort in the task itself. I was fully aware of my actions and fully focused on them. All anxiety about the future or pain about the past began to disappear.

When I finished painting that day, I was alone in a large space that was white of wall, ceiling, and floor. It was there that I settled down at a folding table and chair to the next task that had been left for me. As I stuffed hundreds of envelopes, I developed a rhythmic pattern to my task: flip open the envelope, slip in the paper, run the sponge over the lip, seal—over and over again. The task was menial, but as I scanned the room with my eyes and saw the offices that would become the private treatment rooms, massage rooms, and meeting rooms, I knew that the people who would be walking through these doors to find comfort and help had it much worse than me. They would be dealing with HIV/AIDS, lupus, and cancer. As this registered, I began to feel the shedding of my own desperation. I recognized that my disease was merely a lack of perspective—and although it was snuffing out my spirit and weakening my body, my perspective was definitely something I had the power to change.

Today, I can tell you that the pain I was experiencing and the day in the big, white space were all for a reason. Without that pain, I would not have discovered that I had a calling to help other people and I would not have gone on to spend close to twenty years coaching and counseling others. All of the pain I had experienced had invited growth—and more pain and more growth. And while it's not over yet, the cycle has become less intense over the years. And now, just as the growth is welcomed, the pain can be welcomed too.

As a life coach, and now, more recently, as an interfaith minister as well, I am called on by people to help them heal their lives. "Let me understand my place. That will bring me peace," is something I hear often. I know the longing that comes with those thoughts. There is pain in not seeing a clear path set out before us to follow. There is pain in not feeling valuable or knowing how we are to leave our mark. We want to know we matter. We struggle when we are not recognized or we feel there is nothing particularly outstanding about us. We have egos and we need validation. We need to be witnessed. Like the little kid about to jump off the diving board at the pool saying: "Mom, look at me, look at me!" we never quite outgrow that. We demand evidence of our existence and feel better when we have it.

So what is this mysterious thing called Meaning? Well, it can come in many shapes and sizes, but one thing is for sure: it's something we humans all want. And in today's world our desire for it has taken on a new intensity. Why? Perhaps it's because we can try so many things—there are so many avenues to choose from—it's all too easy to forget what we're looking for. We are confused. We think we're hungry, so we grab something to eat. We think we're bored, so we buy a new toy. We think we're out of touch (good thinking!), so we go to a spiritual retreat (for the weekend, then on Monday we're right back where we started). We grab for quick fixes and nothing sticks. Why? Because we don't realize that what we are yearning for is more integral to our being than any cosmetic improvement can provide.

As I've watched coaching clients piece together the meaningful aspects of their lives, it's been a challenge to help them decipher how to measure meaning. What makes a meaningful relationship with another person? What constitutes meaningful work? Who decides something is meaningful? Is it what is said or done, or rather, how it makes us feel?

I'd answer that meaning is something we feel, more than something we do. Meaning is a state of consciousness. It comes tumbling forth from connection—to ourselves, each other, the earth, spirit, work, or even an inanimate object. A necklace is not meaningful in itself, but when we connect it with the time, place, and person who gave it to us, it takes on a new specialness. It takes on meaning. It enters our consciousness as something precious that we will take care with.

In the empty, white loft I felt connected to myself (versus my pain) for the first time in a long time and I could feel my connection to others even though the place was empty. Meaning was coming into focus. I could feel the hope of the people who would be walking through those doors and I could also feel their pain and frustration. I experienced their innocence as people who did not ask to be ill, but had to navigate that reality. The compassion of the counselors, therapists, and body workers who were poised to serve there was knocking at my own heart as well. The melting of my own armor of numbness was immediate as I allowed myself to connect with the intention to heal that this white space was imbued with. All it took to feel alive with meaning and purpose was that shift in my consciousness. Sustaining that has been a long journey of ups and downs, but once I felt the shift, I've always known how to get it back when I've lost it.

For many, religion is the key to this validation of self. The Old and New Testaments dictate that living a life oriented around God's can provide all the meaning one needs. The third Abrahamic tradition, Islam, puts God (Allah) at the forefront of a meaningful life as well. Buddhism urges its adherents to stop searching for meaning in the material world, believing that the only way to avoid suffering is to cultivate this detachment. Native American cultures teach that true knowledge of the self and compassion for others are the paths to a meaningful life. Every culture has its subtly different translations.

Of all the religions I've studied, the mystic traditions speak to me as being the most relevant to the yearning for meaning in our time. Mysticism proposes a direct connection between us and the force(s) that rule our lives. There is no middleman, doctrine, dogma, or ritual as a prerequisite. But how can this immediacy be felt? Absolute trust and true comfort with "not knowing."

Ah, trust. That's a tricky one these days. All around us, venerable institutions, laws, and constructs for how we operate our lives are crumbling. We no longer know whom to trust to help us guide our course. Our religious institutions, our government, our financial institutions, our corporations, our families, and our schools—these structures don't work their magic the way they used to. I think one of the greatest reasons we grapple for meaning at this particular time is that we're struggling to feel a connection to things we can count on. Yet if we cannot count on the same things we counted on previously, we have no choice but to trust ourselves and that which is less concrete. In other words, we have to have confidence in things that are, at least at first glance, far less monumental.

It is one of the great ironies that while our hunger for a "meaningful" life can be enormous, these days, more and more, our desire for meaning is ultimately satiated by the smaller, quieter aspects of our lives. Meaning is where you look for it—and also *how* you look at it. Meaning is actually all around us, and the circumstances surrounding it can be like an Escher print. Life can look quite meaningless until we focus on a certain point or points and the picture changes. As it comes into focus, we find the peace that discovering meaning can bring.

As I began to write this book, meaning with a big fat capital M flooded my thoughts. But then a series of other M words emerged as well—words like Mystery, Magnificence, and Mind—and in this book I will take you through them in the hopes that they will serve as markers on your path as you continue to search for your own meaning. As my own search evolved and led me to enroll in interfaith seminary, I found clues in the exploration of many religious traditions that will also be drawn upon here to serve you on your way.

How can we hope to find that specific place that is inside each of us where the joy is palpable? There is no easy answer to this question, but one thing is certain: it involves a sense that one's life is meaningful. Meaning solves the mystery even as it deepens it. It brings us home even as it opens infinite landscapes of possibilities. Ultimately, though, it eases the pain.

PART ONE

MYSTERY

It seems that in this modern age in which so much information is immediately accessible to us, is literally at our fingertips, we have lost our reverence for mystery. So easily can we sit down at our computer and Google the answers that we rarely take the time to pause and enjoy the process of discovery. We rarely celebrate the unknown. We think all meaning is in the knowing. In fact, our quest to know often makes it hard to find meaning. Information accelerates life to the point of our being disconnected from things that matter.

In a letter written in 1903, later published in *Letters to a Young Poet*, Rainer Maria Rilke advised:

> *I would like to beg you dear Sir, as well as I can, to have patience with everything unresolved in your heart and to*

try to love the questions themselves as if they were locked rooms or books written in a very foreign language. Don't search for the answers, which could not be given to you now, because you would not be able to live them. And the point is to live everything. Live the questions now. Perhaps then, someday far in the future, you will gradually, without even noticing it, live your way into the answer.

Rilke was addressing a young man, but the same can be said of so many of us, young and old. At the core of our discomfort with this lies the truth that we don't know ourselves very well. When we feel okay within ourselves, we are less impatient for answers. We can find our center and wait. We can tolerate mystery and maybe even revere it. It's just so different from how we've been trained and conditioned to live.

We continue to insist that the outside world reflect something at us that tells us who we are. Whether that comes in the form of success or failure is beside the point. To attempt a meaningful life is to embrace that which can be measured only within ourselves. The yardstick is not our life picture. It is rather how we feel about the person staring back at us in the mirror and how we feel about life.

~ ~ ~

Great Mystery that is life, we ask to be blessed by the conscious knowing that fuels our spirit and makes us live. May we embrace that which we do not understand as well. May we approach all with reverence and know that the answers will come in their own time. May we relish in it and find peace despite the absence of clarity and somehow be comforted by the experience of the mystery that is life itself.

~ ~ ~

ONE

Living in the Gap

Life is a balance between known and unknowns. Space, nature, the inner workings of our bodies—so many aspects of our lives are still mysteries even with all the information we have. Our world's religions have given us explanations. Science has explained what the religions could not and refuted some of what the religions have taught. Yet so much mystery remains. I have found that the more I can relish the mystery, the more meaning I can draw into my life.

Pregnancy comes to mind. I spent both of my pregnancies caught up in a great reverence for the mystery of life. My first time around, no matter how many books I had at my bedside to inform me, there were still so many questions. First, there was the confirmation of the pregnancy.

Then there was the wonder of how I would feel and what life would be like with a baby in it. There was not knowing if the baby was okay until all seemed to check out well. There was feeling the movement of a child inside my belly and yet not knowing what he looked like and who he would be. There were anecdotal warnings of what labor would feel like, but this didn't come close to erasing the acute anticipation of what it would really feel like.

There was also reverence for the natural intelligence of the body. I had no hips on my little, boyish, hundred-pound frame when I became pregnant with my first child. As the pregnancy wore on, my hip bones and back produced excruciating pain as the joints spread to accommodate the growing mass of cells that my body was hosting. During the last trimester, the pain was so bad that I had to roll my gargantuan body out of bed and onto the floor, where I would crawl on my hands and knees to my chosen destination. It took until about eleven a.m. every day to stand up straight.

Unrecognizable to my former self at one hundred fifty pounds, I gave birth to an eight-pound, two-ounce baby boy after a fifty-hour trek through the peaks and valleys of labor. When I was back home, four months of sleep deprivation and hormone-induced emotional toil allowed for a revelation that may seem obvious to those not in my situation: "Oh my God, there is a hip to park this baby on!" All that had been previously unknown had yielded a new "known."

"Isn't Mother Nature amazing?" I thought. "She created a shelf to hold my baby. That's what all that pain was about! And look! I have a second shelf! Maybe I should have another baby!"

And then I had twins (just so my hips wouldn't be jealous of each other). Well, not really, just because after thirty-five, my body got sloppy and dropped two eggs instead of one. All those millions of spermatozoa had two eggs to bombard and I got a boy and a girl out of the deal. Seven pounds each! Not bad. I was in another period of mystery.

"What would it be like to have two?" I wondered. There I was expecting again. Living in the question mark. There were knowns—two babies—one boy, one girl—and the unknown—would they be okay? Could I deliver them myself? Ah, anxiety, mystery's close cousin.

To be fair, of course, there are those that relish mystery. Doctors and researchers, I imagine, revere the mystery as they approach solving it. Artists have to approach an empty canvas or score book and jump into the unknown in order to create. But for a lot of us, the impulse is to hide from that which we don't understand or can't answer. We lose our reverence for mystery, and instead choose fear, avoidance, and denial. It's easier to shut down and close out the unknown rather than enter it with a conscious awareness that we don't have the answers. It is frightening to trust ourselves to be creative, to find answers or resources or people who can help. We avoid that quest, even though it's an opportunity for connection with our essential, creative selves.

In seminary, I learned about the religious traditions of the Yoruba of Nigeria. The Yoruba believe that in issues of material wealth their life is predetermined, so their destiny is just a matter of letting life take its course. They have an opportunity through divination to take steps to improve their character and perhaps positively influence certain outcomes, but ultimately they simply can't know if they are headed to riches or disaster. Their goal then becomes aligning their thoughts and actions with their divine creator, Olorun. Their life is an exercise in patience, as the outcome will become clear only in the end.

Perhaps if we can borrow from the Yoruba tradition and see our destinies as preordained, and therefore largely beyond our influence, we might instead be able to focus on the journey itself. If our goal was to feel bliss, reverence, or love versus to achieve this or that marker of worldly success . . . how would that feel? How would the journey change?

Two years before my husband and I got married, I was still in and out of depression when we traveled to Denali National Park in Alaska. We spent four months working in a dinner show at a resort, and devoted our time off to hiking and exploring the park, which is the size of the state of Massachusetts. It was, and still is, untouched wilderness. Above the tree line, there are few obstructions to huge panoramic views. This made me anxious. This made my husband-to-be excited about walking into the endless possibility of what was out there. I wanted to make plans and chart landmarks so I could feel secure. I needed to *know*. He didn't.

It was an otherworldly feeling to be in such an open space that seemed to have no end. Each time we made our way through this awe-inspiring terrain, I was aware of nothing more than how small and insignificant we were in the grand scheme of things. Walking even felt weird because our eyes lost their depth perception amongst such a vast terrain. The landscape played tricks on us. We were always underestimating how far we were from where we wanted to go.

One morning, we got out of our turtle-shell-shaped tent and got ready to go for a hike. I started to suggest a route I had laid out for us on the map. Mark said we should ditch the map and just see where the day would bring us.

"Gulp." I uttered the cartoonish sound and telegraphed my discomfort. I wanted a destination and a plan to get there.

When I got no reaction from Mark, I took a deep breath and agreed to go with no plan. That day is still one of the highlights of my life.

Shortly after leaving our campsite, I saw the most vibrant, tiny purple flowers, bunched very low along the rocky ground. The Alaskan growing season is very short, so most vegetation stays very low to the ground. The morning dew had settled on the flowers in such a way that they reflected a tremendous amount of light, and it seemed almost as if there was a shower with no source hovering just above their surface. As I marveled at these teeny flowers and beads of water, a little field mouse came to greet me. Maybe he thought I was rare, tall vegetation, because he was not spooked by me, and I can't think of any other reason this creature, which was not conditioned to rely on humans for food, was so calm. It was a quiet meditation to just be with the little creature.

Our next surprise on our day with no plan happened when the afternoon was drawing near and I was getting tired. I sat down to rest as we were climbing to a higher elevation. Mark urged me to get up and keep going, because just ahead of me he had come upon a section of the mountain covered in crystals—geodes and crystal formations just jutting out of the ground. All different shades of white and pink lay spewed across the hill like a treasure that had been dumped there and forgotten. I coveted a little palm-sized geode that looked like a city skyline of crystals perched in a half-moon. I was a city person having a very uncitylike and borderless experience.

I was still tired and looking for a place to plant my butt when Mark had wandered ahead again and then, suddenly, came back into my sight line to announce that I had to climb up to meet him and pronto. I remember each step up to the top of the hilltop was like going up a staircase. I rose higher and higher and it was as if the dust and dirt retreated with each step to reveal a blue sky and clouds at eye level. But more amazing was what waited for us at the end of the land, at the beginning of the sky. About a dozen female Dall sheep and eight or nine baby sheep were quietly relaxing, standing and reclined, along the hilltop. They watched us carefully with their big, brown eyes. The graceful sheep looked like unicorns without horns—mythical figures emanating a knowing that we humans find so hard to obtain.

I finally got to sit down amid these beautiful animals. We must have stayed there close to an hour just floating in a suspended reality as these beauties tolerated us. Their babies roamed freely as the mothers went about their business. None approached us, but none ran away either. It was so quiet that we could not help feeling that we were experiencing a holy encounter, an honor few are permitted.

When we got up to leave and hike back, we saw, up on a ridge on another plateau about a half-mile from us, the rams—the male Dalls. They stay away until mating season. There they were, poised as if smoking cigars while the mothers tended to the babes. We had a chuckle about how female all females are and how male all males are, be they animal or human, and eventually made our way back to our tent.

That day would have never turned out as it did had we followed one of my planned routes. Yet when I fought my desire to control, to know every step of the way, I was able to just enjoy the mystery of our journey. Even in the midst of my depressions, in these magic moments, a reverence for life kicked in. How could it not? I knew it was a lesson I was supposed to be learning: How to live in awe. To live for a feeling instead of a destination and to show up in the present instead of living for a future, perfect plan or lingering in some past regret.

It's understandable that we want order, predictability, and answers to all of our questions. If we have these things, we feel more comfortable. Yet tremendous fullness, aliveness, and a different kind of comfort come when we learn to tolerate the randomness of life. Consider genetic mutation. It is responsible for evolution—for our having things like thumbs and good bacteria that protect us from illness. These are good, useful things. This same process, however, also allows some cells to become malignant. Nothing is neat and tidy. Never has been and never will be.

If everything were linear and predictable, we'd come to a halt. There would be no creativity or evolution or growth. To live is to weave constantly between the known and unknown. Addressing a group of scientists, the Dalai Lama once said: "Curiosity is part of my life, part of my self. Look at this body. Some areas have more hair, some less. Why?" Instead of answering the question, he stopped at the question.

It is this feeling of wonder, openness, and curiosity that can give birth to so much as long as we can get comfortable exploring the vastness of the unanswered questions. Leading life in a meaningful way requires embracing the empty spaces, the blanks and vastness. Living in the gap, we find ourselves.

TWO

Who Am I?

You are not who you think you are.

The mental projections that we have of ourselves are often inconsistent with who we truly are. And, what's worse, the energy and attention needed to preserve this identity can distract us from the meaning we want. We're often in our own way. And even when we do manage to peel away layers of fabricated personality, there is pain. There is death. There is mourning. But if we can linger in this uncertainty—in this mystery—there will be a new dawn.

By 1993, I was fully engaged in my new career, and my dreams of musical theater stardom had been officially relegated to the past. But the switch had not been easy. First came the realization that the results in my career had not been commensurate with my efforts. This was followed by a period of intense mourning in which I recognized the loss of who I thought I was.

"If I'm not onstage, who am I?" I thought. "If I have to admit failure to everyone around me, will I be able to withstand what they think? Who will I be in their eyes? Who will I be in mine?"

A crucial turning point came when I took a quasi-performance-related job to make money. I joined a dance troupe that entertained at large-scale birthday parties and events. At one particular bar mitzvah party, I was a dancing clock. As I moved across the crowded dance floor ensconced in a costume that revealed only my arms and legs, I bawled my eyes out unseen and unheard. It felt so pathetic to be inside this oversize latex clock-contraption as people danced around me to the blaring music and the flashing disco lights. It was surreal that my howls could echo so loudly inside my plastic head while no one on the outside heard them. As long as I kept moving, I seemed like the jolly clock, yet I was living a secret life inside my exaggerated head.

This was not how I thought my dreams and ambitions would play out. And to make things worse, I was unable to see any bright side to the experience (my dancing clock was bringing joy to the party). Instead, I just wanted to go home and curl up in a ball until something changed or I had to pee badly enough to get up. I was losing the ability to fight for my dream and I decided that I had failed.

I had devoted all my time, effort, and money to this dream. How could it not be working out? I had no life outside supporting myself and pursuing my stage ambitions. I chugged day after day through the plan that I had laid out that seemed to work for others on the New York Broadway tract. Why wasn't it happening for me? Who was I if I stopped being this? No more shows to invite people to see. No way to be "seen." No impact to be made. I'd be forgettable. Crash and burn. Failure. Suicide.

Oh, yes, I thought about suicide. I wanted an end and that one seemed as good as any. Depression had set in so gravely that I wished I could carry it out. I would lay in my studio apartment with the lights out and the one window covered, just wishing the end would come because the weight of life was suffocating me. It felt like a boulder sitting on top of me trying to snuff out my last breath. The boulder had me trapped. I couldn't see around it or move it. I didn't see any choices. Somehow, I had enough sense left to do nothing. It just wasn't time. I don't know how, but maybe a part of me somehow knew it was the mourning of an identity and a career and not truly the death of me. Maybe I had learned enough to sense that it was the ego resisting its own death and not really me. Maybe I knew it—some wiser part of myself—that I was going through a milestone in my spiritual growth, although it felt like twenty steps backward in my worldly life. I got through it. I cried, I prayed, I read from "A Course in Miracles,"[1] my bible at the time. I did not speak to anyone about it, which I'd say now was a mistake. Alone, I battled my demons and myself. I could not bear letting anyone know how ugly it was inside my head and what a failure I was. I carried on in my waitressing job and auditions in a fog, barely conscious, but I functioned enough to think I was fooling everyone around me. As Robert Frost says, "The only way out is through," and man, it was ugly.

The field of psychology has attempted to decipher the mysteries of the mind. But beyond egos and superegos, beyond the conscious and unconscious minds, there lies perhaps a higher level of freedom to be found looking through the lens that Buddhists see life through. The Buddha proposes that there is no such thing as the Self, which includes the ego, the mind, and the rest of you. There is just no such thing, according to the Awakened One.

[1] A Course in Miracles is a self-study psycho-spiritual teaching device consisting of three books authored by Helen Schucman and by William Thetford, both professors of psychology at Columbia University College of Physicians and Surgeons.

The four noble truths, the basis for Buddhism, states in its first truth, that all human suffering has a common cause. That cause is attachment. Being attached to a particular result, person, or way of being causes us to suffer when things do not go as we'd hoped or planned. When we don't like how something is, when we fight with reality, we suffer. This is not our true essence. Buddhism, therefore, denies the existence of a self. In Buddhism, there can be no self, no "own being." If there is no self, there can be no attachment, the root of all suffering.

Think about it. We attach to labels, job descriptions, names, status, and a host of other things. We think we are what those around us expect us to be. This is how we arrived at the distorted perception of who we are. We judge our every action—this thing I did was horrible, this thing great. In Buddhism, none of this matters. All is emptiness. Just beingness. This, of course, is really tough for the ego to take!

My case didn't require the giving up of possessions and status symbols because I had none, but it was certainly excruciating to release a self-concept. For many of us this is harder than losing stuff. So many people admired my courage to pursue my dream and they wanted me to win. Many believed I had it all figured out as they observed the discipline, care, and commitment that went into being a singer and performer whose body was her instrument.

From the outside, a bohemian lifestyle seemed exciting and different and tapped into everyone's need to be special, especially mine. To walk away was to telegraph that none of it was true. It was to shatter the image of who I thought I was and watch all the pieces crumble out of a secure frame and onto the floor. The fragmentation between who I was and who was trying to emerge was like having a limb torn off while you're still alive. The trauma was so great that all I wanted to do was sleep. Of course, all of it was an illusion of my own making. No doubt, no one cared as much as I thought they did. But the mental construct was so strong. The ego is so powerful.

Years later I read this passage from *The Healing Wisdom of Africa* by Malidoma Patrice Somé, a shaman of the Dagara tribe of West Africa. It described for me perfectly the transformation I had undergone:

A person's purpose is energetically inscribed in their bones and its actual translation into work should agree with the message engraved in these bones. The question is, what happens when what you do does not align with who you are? It means that you are likely to experience low self-worth, a lack of enthusiasm about what you are doing, and above all, a nagging sense of inner emptiness; In short, an identity crisis. Indigenous people recognize that when the individual does not remember, gradually it is the culture, the society, that forgets.

To shed an entire identity forces us to live in limbo for a time. There is great mystery in that. There is no knowing where you are headed. There is no promise that something better or even good awaits. It's like being pulled through a tunnel in the dark and feeling the seconds as hours as you wait for the end of the ride. When we get out, back in the light, we're blinded by the vastness, but slowly our eyes will adjust and life will come into focus as something new.

Self-grieving is such a painful, lonely, body wracking place. It is so dark and so exhausting. Why would anyone choose to go there? There are only glimpses of meaning until we are on the other side of it. No wonder most of us try to avoid it. We are afraid we'll never come back from it, so we won't go there, and yet going there and getting through to the other side can be one of the most transformative experiences life can offer.

We are not the pain. We are not the tragedy. We are the soul and the soul is eternal. And the experience of the soul lives on as wisdom to relieve suffering for others.

We are not who we think we are. Thank goodness.

THREE

Success Happens

A woman walks into her kitchen after a long day at work, to find chaos *everywhere*. Her teenagers are glued to the TV, pizza boxes and soda cans are strewn across the counters. "Has anyone started their homework?" she asks, knowing the answer in advance. She's not one to talk, though. Her life is a mess. Bills are a week late—not because she doesn't have the money, but because she's so busy managing she's barely functioning. Climbing the corporate ladder has helped her fall a few rungs in her home life. Piles of dirty clothes lie in her bathroom. She hasn't cooked a meal in weeks and she's had to change her kids' parent/teacher meetings twice. She could hire someone, but why pay someone when she can do it herself? Success happens.

A man is starting a second family with his new, younger wife. He swears he'll put his family first by being present and accounted for and not by only being the provider. His previous marriage ended when his ex-wife kicked him out of their home when she discovered he was having an affair. She got a handsome alimony and child-support agreement to provide for their four kids. His late nights at the office and extensive travel estranged him from his spouse until they barely spoke and he felt compelled to get his needs met elsewhere. He wants to make up for his past mistakes and thinks he now has the chance to do that. But he is already slipping into past routines. Success happens.

A single parent works two jobs to make ends meet and wonders if she should just stop paying the babysitter and give up one of the jobs, but the math just doesn't work itself out. She works until she can barely see straight and then comes home to tidy up and feed the kids. As she studies for an undergraduate degree (all expenses paid by her job) until one a.m. and gets only four hours of sleep a night, life has become one big race to the finish line that seems to never come. Success happens.

All stories are different, but really, they are all the same. Getting what we want seems to come with a price. The more money we make, the more money we have to make. The better the job, the more it demands. And so on. We're a tired bunch. We move like lightning to fulfill the obligations of our day. With our nose to the grindstone, jumping through all the hoops of modern life (neatly or not), making our way systematically through the benchmarks that are expected, we lose track of the richness that we hoped our efforts would achieve. The richness is there, but we are preoccupied. We've invented a man-made state called success, and we are so entrenched in managing it that we wear ourselves thin. We become blind to what we hoped it would create. I have noticed a trend with clients and others in my life—and in my own life, in fact—success finally comes, but at a cost. What is the meaning?

During my interfaith seminary training we studied the Hindu scriptures and these ancient words got at the root of our human predicament with a simplicity and clarity that I had not seen before.

Hinduism asserts that there are two sets of human desires. There are four worldly desires, but there are three *true* desires. According to an interpretation by Huston Smith, an authority of the world's religions, the four desires that humans chase in this world are: pleasure, worldly success, duty, and liberation. Pleasure is a natural instinct that we are hardwired for. We reach for pleasure to avoid pain. As we mature, our self-interest grows to include worldly success. The third desire we chase is to serve in some way, which is often still rooted in the desire for recognition. Finally, we want liberation from all that blocks us from what we truly desire.

That brings me to Hinduism's three true desires: Infinite Being, Infinite Knowing, and Infinite Bliss. Although we chase the four desires, it's the three desires we truly wish to satisfy. This smoke-and-mirrors illusion of worldly success is what trips us up. We want and we want and we want. But we don't know what it is we want. We create societal rituals and benchmarks to reach and yet forget their true meaning and purpose.

When we got engaged, Mark and I were actors, each working second jobs. When he asked me to marry him, he presented me with a sparkly peridot ring with two tiny diamond chips on either side, mounted on the most delicate ribbon of gold, which fit my finger beautifully. Peridot, a semiprecious stone, is the August birthstone and, for us, represented the month in which we met.

I could see how people's faces dropped when they asked to see the ring, and I would splay out my fingers at the end of my outstretched arm and beam at them.

"Oh, that's different," they would say. Or, "That's pretty." Or some such perfunctory comment. I knew they expected something else, but I loved my ring and would not be shamed into feeling that it, he (Mark), I, or we were "less than" for it.

My mother was bent out of shape about me not having a diamond. She offered to buy me one. I was surprised that she was so emphatic about it, but I wasn't at all tempted by her offer. It would have been an emasculating thing to do, and I honestly did not care about the diamond ring. I wanted Mark.

As the years went on, the subject of a diamond would come up every now and then. However, every time there might have been money to buy a diamond, we were too practical to do so. The first time, we built a deck on our home instead, and then we were blessed with three children who needed all kinds of things, including destroying the deck to add on to our house when our twins came along. The list of things that were more important than a ring went on. It just wasn't that important, nor did I need to have one to fit in or prove something. So it was very odd that recently, as I stood in my local jeweler's store, I put money down on the very bauble I had rejected so often before.

It's not an extravagant ring. It has a brilliant .7-karat diamond in the middle of two heavy bands, one yellow gold, the other white, fused together in perfect symmetry with a smattering of tiny diamonds exploding out from the center as if fireworks erupted as it was being made. It's not an engagement ring, but worn on the left ring finger it certainly telegraphs that I am betrothed.

I had been looking at this particular ring for seven years, ever since my twins were born. I would "visit" it when I was in the store getting batteries put in watches or buying a gift for someone. I felt very foolish behaving as if I was going to buy this ring and time after time walking out without it. It was embarrassing because the jeweler is also a neighbor and I wondered if he thought I was just a flake or just a wannabe diamond owner. Anyway, several months ago, when I was visiting "my" ring, Robert, the jeweler, was excited to show me a gorgeous diamond he had come across on his weekly trip to New York City's Diamond District. It was the shiniest diamond I had ever seen. My first reaction was to tell him it would look amazing in my ring, which then had a much tinier diamond in it. He got all excited and pulled the ring out of the display case and showed me with his delicate tools how it would sit in the middle of the bands. I told him on the spot that I wanted it. The move seemed so impulsive and out of character for me that I started getting nervous and asked him to call me with the price so I could get away and think about why I really wanted it.

After all these years, was I succumbing to a buried desire for a "proper" diamond?

Had the meaning that society had anointed to the diamond engagement ring finally become my own?

After asking myself what my motivation was for buying the ring, it was clear that it had nothing to do with social expectations. I simply liked the ring. And buying it for myself was a stake in the ground in the difficult financial times after 9/11. It symbolized personal freedom and a lack of fear. It has come to represent my life with Mark and my love for our family; two people (two bands) joined by one brilliant stone (love) and surrounded by tiny shimmering lights (our children). It means something more to me than an engagement ring might have seventeen years ago.

We really do essentially want more from life than possessions, status, and a list of social milestones to achieve. I can say that is true for most people, but what brings many of us to that realization is that the trap of success seems less satisfying when we recognize that it centers meaning on the self. Fulfilling our material wish list can often become too small of a goal to create lasting enthusiasm. The chase becomes boring after a while. Hinduism teaches that since we are creatures that can imagine a future without us in it, we long to have more to leave behind than a trail of things that can't fit into our final resting spot with us. We want to know we have mattered and left out mark and yet somehow we've been fooled into thinking that a certain level of success—often equated in our minds with stuff and privilege—is the prerequisite.

When we choose to stop worshipping the false idol of worldly success, it is not an agreement to be poor, but it does require the discipline to stay in touch with ourselves and not be sucked in by what the world still defines as success. It can be like living as an alien in our own country. There is a certain amount of isolation that is needed until we can withstand the ignorance of others toward the new culture we are assimilating. We can't expect people to understand why we've sold our gorgeous home or given up a six-figure salary or rejected the chance at a formal education. When we are on a whole other operating system, we will butt up against conventional thinking and what we have come to call logic.

There was a time in my life when I had made a pact with a force greater than I that struck me as being very close to bargaining for Hinduism's three true desires. While I was waiting on tables and pursuing a musical theater career, I did so with such a vengeance that I had deprived myself of romantic love, friendships, fun, and even a healthy weight, since my brain forgot to reset itself once anorexia and bulimia set in. It was all in the name of "making it" in New York City, and I wore my discipline and perfectionist tendencies as a shield of my-shit-don't-stink-dom. I was superior. As I've said earlier, I wanted people to think that success had happened, but inside, although I was independent and paying my own bills, I felt like a failure because my dreams stubbornly would not take the shape I wanted them to.

Eventually, I crashed and burned, and after a three-year dark period I was finally seeing some light. The big, white loft helped as well as an attempt by my parents to have me admitted to what today would be called a rehab center. When the admitting doctor confirmed that my behavior and dark thoughts merited being checked in, I literally fled and scared myself straight. It was then that I made the deal. I stopped begging God and the ethers to be successful in my career and started praying to know happiness, peace, and love. If I had these three things, I knew, deep down, that I would have a way to navigate life that was not as painful as the one I had chosen until then.

If I had happiness, I'd not expect anything worldly to take its place. If I had peace, it would not matter how much money I made or what I did for a living. And if I had love and learned to love, I would be enriched, if not rich itself. Although the deal was not an instant cure to my ills, it was the basis of my recovery. My life turned around dramatically. I found love. Or maybe it is more accurate to say, I recognized love because Mark was already in my life routing for me. I found a new career. A period of prosperity came too. There are definitely days where I forget the rebirth that occurred upon the making of that pact. But when I forget, I get back to it, and the path is made straight again. Once I am back in touch with what matters, the meaning becomes clear. Patience is easier to come by and priorities fall into place. As a recovering perfectionist, I can extol the virtues of peace of mind over perfection and I highly recommend it.

I find it important to know what matters and what can wait. We need to know when to stop and recharge and that requires prioritizing and reprioritizing in every moment. Things that wait have to be tolerated or hired out for someone else to do. A messy house and late bills are not crimes against humanity, although they sound less than ideal. Rising heart attack rates and stress-related illness do seem like irresponsible crimes against our bodies and ourselves when their underlying causes can be stopped.

Believe it or not, when people who are amazed at how I "do it all" (run a business, write books, travel, manage a family and a marriage, care for a home) ask me, "How do you *do* it?" I first tell them that I have no magic formula and that things are probably not as perfect as they make them out to be. Then I tell them it was my years of waitressing that trained me to be excellent at prioritizing. I'm not joking. For twelve years of my life I waited on tables (I started in high school). That's a lot of prioritizing. That's a lot of mental practice. It's completely second nature now to know what can wait and what has to be done right away.

"Drinks and bread will hold that table while I get the desserts for the other table. Cappuccinos take forever to make, so before you disappear into that kitchen, get water for table 2 or tell the busboy to do it. While you're going to the bar, pick up extra straws for the cranky couple and lemons for the lady with the tea."

Those years were an exercise in consolidating effort and thinking on your feet. As the Israelis require military service from their youth, I think we should put all young people to work waiting on tables. They'll learn to prioritize and they'll never be condescending to another human again. Maybe it's not as patriotic as serving in the military, but certainly a public service to the spiritual growth of our youth.

What's clear is that if we want better for our youth and ourselves it's fair to say there has never been a guarantee that when success happens we'll know joy—the truest desire, according to the Hindus. However, to know joy is to feel connected. To be connected allows us to find meaning, that which can truly last forever.

PART TWO

MINISTER

To minister: To give aid or service. To minister: To tend to another holding the space for their divinity and innocence to shine through.

The first definition is from *Webster's*, the second is mine. It is a transaction between human beings. It means taking care of another and I would certainly argue that one does not need a degree or an ordination to be able to do it. As an interfaith seminary student, it was a revelation that one doesn't need to talk about God or religion to minister to someone effectively. Of course, one can if they want to share that common language with someone, but if they do not or cannot, the service can still matter greatly. All that is asked is that you are really there—that you listen intently and give of your time, attention, and soul.

The synergy of ministry is not limited to humans. Many feel

ministered to by their animals, and the earth requires us to be ministers and shepherds to its well-being as well. And one other thing that can easily be overlooked: when we are ministering to people, we have to remember to minister to ourselves as well, so we can keep functioning in a way that we are able to actually give of ourselves effectively. The results of this work if it is done correctly? It heals both parties. It also helps two people together discover meaning in even the most tragic circumstances.

Our true destiny is not to be ministered unto but to minister to ourselves and to our fellow men.

—Franklin D. Roosevelt

~ ~ ~

Energy of All Things, allow me the blessing of a full heart that I may have more than enough of myself to share to another who needs it. May I be a blessing to anyone that comes my way. May I have the patience to care and the strength to lend. May I see the light of life in all who are put in my path. Help me to see it, embrace it and give it. May I serve as it is called for. Thank you. And so it is.

~ ~ ~

FOUR

To Minister

Jewish boys don't ride motorcycles, and Jewish girls don't become ministers. At least that's what my mom said. But my brother owns a Harley and I've become an interfaith minister. My Jewish father doesn't quite know what to make of it, so he calls me Mother Superior, to which I just respond with a smile.

My journey to becoming ordained was a delicious gift to myself. Although I consider myself to be an ongoing student of life, to be a student in a dedicated setting was a wonderful indulgence. Stuffing myself with as much reading, meditating, pondering, questioning, arguing, discussing, experiencing, and sharing was one of the richest, most mind-expanding experiences I have had. But the gem of it all was less about the studying and religious education and more about the internal shift in me. Before I started the process both the noun "minister" and the verb "to minister" interested me. What would it feel like to be said noun, a "minister"? Once I was ordained, however, I forgot there was a noun to it all. To minister is what I learned how to do, and it was one of the most important things I ever learned.

Ministering is what I believe people are longing to do for each other and to have done to them. To minister is to connect to the deepest humanity of the human being. It is to join them at their purest, essential being and hold their goodness as the container for their life. To join people here is to find compassion for their every drop of suffering. To meet others in the pool of conflict and help them find their way out to wholeness—this is the crux of ministering, and it's where the deepest meaning can be found, because when people remember that they are whole, their connection to self and all reignites. Can we do the same thing for our neighbor by meeting over a cup of coffee? Yes.

The messy part is when God gets into the mix. We have to tiptoe to find whether we are talking to a believer or not and, if it is a believer, what brand of believing is involved Being an equal-opportunity "interfaith" minister who has a general knowledge of the world's major religions evened out the playing field for me. It's like speaking many languages and picking and choosing among them the words that best describe the situation instead of being limited by any one of them.

By going to seminary, I also had the singular experience of watching people's reaction to me change completely. As if I had the point of view of a movie camera's lens, I stood still and watched as people reacted all around me. They stopped swearing (or apologized if they did). They also held their breath waiting for me to judge them or react to them differently from how I would have reacted before. And perhaps most intimidating of all: they expected me to be wiser. It was like being in the Twilight Zone. Had I turned into an alien visiting from space? Did I sprout tentacles? Had I grown wings and a halo? God, no. But I learned a lot. I learned that when people hear the word "minister," they often go into a protective armor against any religious wounding they've experienced. Their hackles go up. They think I might try to convert them to some way of thinking. Or, on the other hand, they melt into the comfort of expectation in the minister being a conduit for the divine. The way I see it, everyone is a conduit to the divine and sometimes we need a little help so we go to the good rebbe or priest or pastor or minister, someone who is more practiced in connecting to a larger source. Where we get into trouble is in handing all our power over to another *human being*, expecting them to be the ultimate deliverer of truth. That's how the abuse of power is given birth to.

Ministering therefore works best as a form of caring and connecting—a witnessing of another in whatever situation they find themselves in. To minister is to connect with the human qualities in each of us. We crave that and our work is to create it in our lives ourselves. It's one of the most potent and readily available ways to connect with meaning.

I remember the day I became a minister (noun). It wasn't my ordination or graduation. It was a year or so before that. It was a perfectly ordinary day where I had the usual mix of activity: working, running a few errands before the kids got out of school, and chauffeuring them to their extracurricular activities. I stopped into my local seamstress's shop to pick up something she had tailored for me. I swooshed in the door with cheer, looking forward to seeing Lola. But Lola was not in the mood to joke around as she usually did.

Lola's in her sixties, with a glorious head of salt-and-pepper hair tied back in a ponytail. She wears huge black-framed glasses that she's probably had since 1985 and that overpower her little face, a face I can see as an echo of the mischievous girl she was when she was young. Now, later in her years, her face is still tiny with a hint of fire in her eyes, but the body has slowed from sitting at her sewing machine and spread beyond a girly shape.

"Oh, Lora," she says in her thick Italian accent, with a forlorn look on her face.

"My mother—she died. In Italy."

"I'm so sorry," I said.

"My sisters, my mother, I have not seen in twenty years. I don't know if I should go," she said, searching my eyes as if the answer was locked behind them.

Lola splayed out the problem for me as if putting out a deck of cards on the counter that separated us. She talked, and I moved right into "coach mode." By that I mean that after seventeen years of coaching people from problem to solution, my normal approach is to ask questions and help people unlock their own answers and dissipate their confusion. As soon as I got out a question or two, it hit me.

"This is not a coaching scenario, just listen," my thoughts commanded me.

The minister is a witness to the human experience. And that day, I got it. I just listened to Lola. I just allowed her to get it all out. When she did, she looked at me for a final word.

"Do what will bring you peace," I said, and we were done.

As I got back into my car, just six feet from the front door of Lola's store, I knew that I had crossed over some kind of marker, but instead of feeling celebratory, I just cried. It wasn't Lola's pain I was feeling, and I wasn't experiencing anything negative. I was humbled. I cried with gratitude that Lola had needed something I could give her, even if I wasn't sure what it was.

Life soon provided me with more practice. Later on the same day, my oldest child, Skyler, had a Cub Scout outing to the local firehouse. As the boys got a chance to climb inside the equipment and interact with the firemen, I pulled back to a spot where I could stand and take in the whole scene. I didn't realize I was standing next to Sue, one of the other moms, until she turned to me out of the blue and told me that her brother has MS.

"Oh," I said. "Is it advanced?"

"Yeah, it's really bad," she said. "It's come on hard and fast."

"Are you the primary caretaker?"

"His wife left him. I was a nurse before I stopped working, so it makes sense that I do it. He's probably going to have to move in with me. It's just horrible," she said. All of this was said without our looking at each other. We were facing out, watching the boys as they became short of breath in the excitement of having a firsthand experience with machinery. All of a sudden Sue turned to me.

"I can't believe I'm telling you all this," she said, embarrassed.

"It's okay. I can handle it. I'm training to be a minister," I said. The words just came out of my mouth before my mind could edit them. I thought I must have sounded so stupid, but she got what I meant and lost her embarrassment and continued to share with me about her situation.

Okay, I was getting it, I was getting this minister thing. "Just listen. Just be. Just witness. Just care. You don't have to fix it." I needed to go to seminary to learn what a lot of people do naturally. Call me thick.

But that was not the last confirmation of the day, there was one more. When I got home from the Cub Scout outing, my husband had his monthly poker game going on at the house. Joe was the last of his poker guys to come in. He, his wife, and their twin daughters adopted from China had been our neighbors, but they had since moved away. Although a trim and good-looking man, Joe was never spry. He had bad knees and moved rather slowly. On this night, he was particularly heavy in his gait and I could tell he was dragging himself along. I just looked at him until words formed in my mouth.

"What's the matter?"

"Andre died," he said. Andre was his beloved white Grand Pyrenees dog.

It was the first time I'd seen tears in Joe's eyes.

"Oh, Joe," I said, as I came to hug him.

It was a short cry, but this is a man who I've seen endure a construction accident that required having his jaw wired shut for months and the emotional roller coaster of infertility and adoption without shedding a tear, and he had lost the dog that saw him through those obstacles and many more. He was bereft.

Joe shook it off and went down to the basement for the poker game. I turned to go back to baking brownies with the kids (a poker game tradition), and a strange peace came over me. I had somehow done the right thing just being there for Joe. No profound words or guidance needed. There was no effort. I knew there was some kind of initiation going on. I felt it. I accepted it. I even understood it, on some level beyond words.

A question emerged for me: "Is ministering something you turn on and off or is it a constant way of being?" My first reaction was that only those on a straight course to sainthood could make it a constant way of being. The rest of us are human, and humans have emotions and make mistakes. There are going to be situations that annoy us or anger us and people whom we just can't fathom "being" with, much less looking at. It's okay. It's okay.

Then there are those people who are always taking care of others. There are extraordinary people with a constant ability to give and love, no matter what. Bless them. That ain't me, but I'm working on it.

I also know from my experience in the coaching profession that there are a lot of people who minister to others to avoid ministering to themselves. In other words, they give from an empty cup rather than give from a cup that is overflowing. They don't do their own personal growth work to heal their own wounds. Instead, they avoid their own pain by tending to the pain of others. That may sound noble, but to truly give freely, we have to know how to give to ourselves as well. That doesn't mean pampering ourselves with surface comforts, but rather having the capacity to fill our own being with love and forgiveness. "Physician, heal thyself" (Luke 4:23). That is wholeness and that is a healthy place to minister from. It requires the balance of a sound self and an outstretched arm to the next person.

Yet even before we are healed, it is possible to find that judgment-free, loving connection with anyone if you dig deep enough into the well of compassion that dwells in every person. My graduating class from seminary taught me that.

The diversity in my class was beyond any I had ever been exposed to in one room: Vietnam vets, cops, a cantor, Wicca devotees, Christians, Cherokee descendants, social workers, a Buddhist nun, blacks, whites, Hispanics, Asians—you name it, we had it. It was a challenge to stay open and it was disappointing to see myself struggle with my own prejudices. I had to fight my own ego into submission for the first few classes because I would make assumptions about who I was on a par with or not in terms of professional experience. (What a waste and how wrong I was!) Yet in that classroom, there was an understanding. "We are here to see each other as whole, divine creatures and act accordingly." For the most part we did. It was humbling. And we learned. We learned that you can find the good in everyone. We learned that everyone, no exceptions, has been through something that they've had to overcome to still be here. We learned that every life story is special and unique and yet totally inconsequential because the true journey is getting back to your Self. No matter how, no matter what. That's the work. To get back to love.

Yes, to minister to one another is to get back to love. That's why we crave it. To be held as whole and complete the way a loving mother sees her child. No matter the wrinkles, bumps, and bruises, we want someone to see us for who we really are. As our world has sped up, we have gotten further and further away from seeing each other. People can appear to us as just bumpers in the pinball game of life. We bump off them getting to where we need, or think we need, to go. But when we minister to one another, or even to ourselves, we stop and soak up what's good, what's real. It's there; it's really there. Jew, Christian, Muslim, Buddhist, Taoist, Hindu—at the core, the human soul is the same and the human heart wants to pump its muscle so we can know we are alive. To minister is to actively love. Therein lies the meaning. It always comes back to love.

FIVE

Giver of Life

It was a stormy night in New Jersey, and it was not unusual for at least one of my children to jump into bed with me to have their fear of thunder and lightning quelled by the closeness of a parent. On this night in July, however, all three of them were huddled on my bed, begging me to help them cope. I had not gone to bed yet, and they were still alert because sleep had barely had a chance to lull them when the storm got loud.

As my heart smiled and I reveled in the cuteness of my little flock taking cover around me, I looked up through a big cutout window high above my bed and got fearful myself. The summer sky had turned black and yellow and the trees were not blowing in one direction or another. The tops of the trees were swirling in a circular motion.

I did not like what I saw one bit, so I gathered my sheep and as I crossed my husband in the hallway I informed him that we needed to get out of that room and into the basement.

"It's not a tornado, for God's sake," he said. "We're not in Oklahoma."

"Fine," I snapped back. "But let's get into the old part of the house."

The old part of my house, built in 1940 with plaster walls, is solid. The new part, added in 2001, of today's cardboardlike materials, made me uneasy. I wanted us in the hardy part of the home. All five of us sat on my older son's twin bed and watched a formidable lightning display that lit up the sky like the Macy's Fourth of July fireworks show. It did not seem real.

We were not in our new shelter more than three minutes when a huge crash shook the whole house. A tree had hit the room we had just left. It pushed in the walls both upstairs in my bedroom and downstairs. Five inches to the left, it would have hit my window and landed on top of the bed and me and the kids if we had stayed put.

So much for there being no tornadoes in New Jersey. A five-mile radius had been hit by a microburst, which is an upside-down tornado. Hundreds of trees were down. Cars and houses smashed, but not a single fatality or injury. Driving around the next day was like navigating a war zone as cars tried to find alternate routes around gigantic trees and downed electric cables. The insurance folks were out in droves assessing dozens of damaged homes. There was no precedence for this in our area.

Two things came out of that night for me. One, I can trust my intuition. I already knew that, but this event drummed it home. I knew we needed out of that room despite that appearing to be an overreaction on my part. The other, don't mess with Mother Nature! She has the ultimate power, and a reverence for her is a must. She who "giveth" life also "taketh away."

Al Gore has said: "We are witnessing a collision between our civilization and the Earth." I saw a collision between my house and a tree. I get it. Freak weather patterns tell us something is afoot, that we are not in Kansas anymore. Tornadoes in New Jersey?

Our lack of consciousness where our environment is concerned is another place where we choose separation over connection. We act as if the environment were meaningless to us. We have separated ourselves from that which sustains us and, as a result, lost the balance of give-and-take that it requires. We have until lately (and many persist) taken the environment for granted. It seems that we have been lulled into believing that the earth and her resources have been here only to serve us and that she requires nothing in return. We are now being called to minister to the planet. She needs our attention and our appreciation so that we may return to a peaceful coexistence with her. If we don't, the earth will no longer be able to give and we will no longer be able to take. "As the separation between human being and the earth widens, so do the chances of our survival lessen."[1]

In the 1970s there was a public-service announcement on TV designed to teach us not to litter and throw garbage out of our car windows. It featured a Native American man in full feather headdress standing by the side of the road with one stoic tear rolling down his face. Today that image would be far from politically correct, but it made an impression on me and I never forgot it. Just because we learned to stop littering from our cars (mostly in large part due to fines we would receive if we didn't!) doesn't mean we stopped that abuse of Mother Earth. As we are now entering a stage where being "green" is in—conserving energy and nature—these seemingly small actions matter

[1]Linda Clarkson, Vern Morrissette, and Gabriel Regallet, *Our Responsibility to the Seventh Generation: Indigenous Peoples and Sustainable Development* (Winnipeg, Canada: International Institute for Sustainable Development, 1992).

a lot to the whole of what we have to heal. If we are patient and tune in to the earth, it can be a meaningful exchange. We are being called to be conscious.

I am not a tree hugger per se. I have only one houseplant that has survived my touch, I put on makeup before hiking and wear the latest Merrell boots when I go into the wilderness, for God's sake, but I do believe that we can have a relationship with our natural surroundings that is more significant than mere circumstance.

I was running in my local park on the day that we were doing some particularly interesting work on Native American traditions in my seminary class. I could not make it to class that day because of a family commitment. I was torn and wished I could have been in both places at once. As I took a run that morning, a large, speckled hawk swooped right by my head. I only saw it out of the corner of my eye, but I had the distinct feeling that the bird was trying to get my attention. On the second time around, the hawk came down from its perch and suspended itself, wings flapping in my direct path. I had to stop. I felt there was no coincidence that a hawk was in my path on the day I was missing the visit of Grandmother Sara, an elder from the Mohawk Tribe, Iroquois Nation, to our class.

With no one around but the hawk and me, I asked it what it wanted to tell me. I did not hear any words or language, but I sensed that the hawk was my substitute teacher. It was ministering to me. It was somehow taking care of me. It was making sure I did not miss the gist of the class by coming along to engage me. I later found out that I was quite right. The subject of that day's class was indeed the importance of feeling a connection with nature. I am not suggesting we become Dr. Doolittle and start talking to the animals, but we could all benefit from being more in tune with our natural world. Many Native and earth-based traditions have rituals that evoke the four elements: earth, wind, fire, and water. If we gave just two minutes of thought to these on a daily basis, perhaps we could cultivate a reverence for them that would enable us to be more conscious of the earth's needs.

There is no question that we have been at least very shortsighted in how we deal with our natural resources. We have always believed in unlimited resources, which in a way is good, positive, forward-facing thinking. Yet on the other hand, we have lost our perspective on the generational impact we make.

In many Native American cultures, to this day, no decision is made without consideration of the seven generations that will come after and the impact the decision will have on them. There is also consideration for how the seven generations that preceded them would feel about their actions. That is respect and consciousness. As a culture that pays money to drink water, one of nature's most abundant resources, out of plastic bottles, we have fallen short here. We have numbed ourselves from feeling the weight of our actions. We have cut ourselves off from meaning by not measuring the impact of our actions when it comes to our relationship with the greatest giver of life, the earth. When we minister to the earth as Mother Nature ministers to us by feeding us and providing for us, we reach the natural balance that was intended. When we take too much and do not give back, we disrupt the equilibrium. Just like a human relationship that has too much "me, me, me," it suffers until it gets back to "we."

Very slowly, we are being drawn to, and perhaps by necessity, a "we" perspective versus a "me" perspective—examining Female versus Male. It is that female nurturing embrace that is being called forth now. It is an invitation to connect with the earth's pulse. We are being invited to renew a meaningful exchange with a living, breathing thing. To minister to the earth now means going beyond the surface level to a deeper place where we really listen to her and the creatures that rely on her for sustenance, us included.

Indigenous cultures have a lot to teach us in terms of maintaining a deep reverence for the earth and all the bountiful gifts she supplies. Perhaps this is in large part because they have relied, and in many parts of the world they continue to rely, on the land to survive and so have no choice but to follow the cycle of the earth and cycle of the seasons. In our modern Western societies, we can override the seasons. We have comforts such as air-conditioning that can keep us out of sync with nature's demands. That's not to say that we shouldn't enjoy these comforts, but it is to point out that we have stopped listening to the very source of our survival and have become out of contact with the give-and-take Mother Nature requires. When we are disconnected, we lose opportunities for meaning.

I have a Dutch friend who brings a deep reverence for the earth into her life daily. She presented me with an interesting challenge. She and her children ride their bikes to school almost every day. She was responsible for a town motion to prohibit school buses from idling in front of the schools, emitting horrible fumes into the air and wasting fuel. She also prides herself on putting out just one can of garbage for collection per week for her family of five. Since my family of five puts out at least three cans of garbage for disposal per week, with her encouragement, I tried to reduce our waste. It was a tough undertaking. We did not get down to one can but we did cut it in half by reusing more containers, recycling more, and trying to buy things that had less packaging—especially food.

Our culture loves its food in pretty packages, just as much as we do other consumer goods. It's simply another layer of separation we put between the earth and ourselves because multibillion-dollar marketing has become our ruler. At farmers' markets we buy our food in the package nature intended for it, itself. We may put it in a bag to carry but we touch it, feel it, smell it, and sometimes take a taste when no one is looking. But the way we decorate our food so we are more attracted to buying it is crazy, and our need to be seduced to buy this or that gets us so far off track from what matters—eating it! When cooked pasta and sauce were packaged to be assembled for consumption by the completely culinarily challenged, I knew we had hit a new low. When I pay attention to what I am putting in my mouth, the raised consciousness that it requires makes food a meaningful experience. When I know I am putting clean, healthy food into my body, it's as if I feel the nourishment reaching out to all the parts of my body through my bloodstream. I feel the connection between the land that supplied the food and myself. Even an indulgence of delicious taste sensations that are not particularly healthy can create a sensual experience with food, meaningful or not.

The whole separation of ourselves from the planet that feeds us is evident in the farming industry in this country. Through the decades, the industry has become just that—an industry. The family farm has been a tougher and tougher model to sustain. Not profitable, the land that was being farmed became more valuable than the crops that could potentially be produced. Government started to make it more profitable for farmers *not* to grow food, so that's what many of them did to pay the bills. It's also hard to stomach that only 2 percent of the food grown in the United States is grown organically. The sales revenues for organic food have gone up 20 percent every year for the last decade, but there is a lot of room to go before it is our predominant way to grow food. Business again controls the game on this. It is expensive to grow organically because it requires more manual labor to work the soil without chemicals and there is more loss of food. (Ministering takes time!)

My local pizza shop and bagel store recently posted a sign about their need to charge more money to their customers due to the wheat shortage they are facing. A fifty-pound bag of flour went from eighteen dollars to fifty-five dollars in one month's time. Supposedly, there is no shortage of food in the world, but there have been droughts in several of the large exporting countries.

Furthermore, many wheat fields became valuable real estate for growing corn for ethanol—a higher-profit commodity right now. I can't say these droughts are directly related to our environmental challenges, since there were droughts long before we abused the planet. We are still not globally the best managers of our resources, however. People are hungry in other countries and people still go hungry in the United States. We are not ministering to them by caring for and distributing what we do have.

I wonder if wheat will remain sparse as my kids grow up. I worry that my kids and grandchildren will have to live in houses covered by a glass bubble to keep the environment livable for humans. I wonder if they'll be able to enjoy the beach or a swimming pool in thirty years or if the government will ban them because the surgeon general warns that sun exposure could cause death.

What would the seventh generation have to say about that?

SIX

They Came for You

Not many people will argue that having children in their lives, whether they be their grandchildren or nieces and nephews or the little neighbor next door, help bring meaning into their lives. A smile, a tug at your heart, a warm fuzzy feeling, a sense of being useful and purposeful. But when they are ours, and it's forever, we realize there is more to it. They push our buttons, they challenge us, and they teach us. How dare they? What if every child's meaning in our life represents a lesson? What if they are here not just for us to take care of them, to watch over their growth, but to be ministers themselves to our growth as adults?

A friend of mine lost her full-term baby boy just days before her due date; he was strangled by the umbilical cord. She had to deliver him. It was an incomprehensible loss. The grief was overwhelming. She mourned, slowly moved on, and two years later gave birth to a beautiful daughter, who was followed by another daughter three years after that. The mother still thought about her first child and wondered what the meaning was of his brief existence. Then one night, her elder daughter looked at her before bed and whispered:

"You know, Mom, sometimes I feel like I have a big brother in heaven watching out for me."

The daughter had not been told about her brother. The mother found it somehow comforting that her daughter felt a connection to a brother she interpreted to be the son she had lost. As much as she wished it had not happened, my friend wonders whether she'd have her precious daughters if her first baby had lived. Some meaning in her tragic loss now comes from the thought that in some way her first child died to make way for the rest. He had done all he had come to do and left earlier than anyone would have liked. She finds peace in this answer for herself. She has created her own meaning from her loss.

The loss of a child carries a pain I cannot imagine enduring, but so many have had to and do. The stretch that it takes to find a meaning in that loss is huge, but once one can take that leap, healing is possible. Moving forward can occur.

Something that I find comfort in, and that I've shared when I am called on in a more ministerial capacity, is that souls make contracts with each other.

"Okay. I'll come into the world as your child. I'll die in my twenties, which will devastate you, but your growth and your contribution to those around you with the foundation you'll create in my name will be your life's work and the real reason I came into your life."

If our souls precede our bodily existence and come together for mutual growth, the embodiment of parent and child is a pact for growth. While our children certainly bless our lives, it takes work to stay conscious and mindful to what they may be calling forth in us. It's so easy to retreat into our own pain and worry. After all, it can be very hard to have other beings depending on us at every turn. As I say to my friends who don't have kids and want to know what it's like: "Imagine working in an office where no one can do anything or make any decisions without you. They constantly interrupt you and you have no control over your time. Imagine you had to be part of their every move, including going to the bathroom!" That usually registers a reaction somewhere between awe and horror. Yes, it's hard to be a parent.

If we are not taking care of ourselves, it is easy to get overwhelmed by our dependents' needs and be quick to anger. I call this "Mommy rage" or "Daddy rage." Others may go into overdrive, eager to please and take care of their flock only to find themselves lost when children are gone. It takes a lot of work to take care of ourselves too so we can give from fullness instead of from an exhausted emptiness. We need to minister to ourselves, to heal old wounds instead of trying to pretend they are not there. It is when we are full and not leaking out our goodness through our wounds that we can stay conscious and see above the chaos to find meaning.

Each of my children has ministered to me. How? Mainly in the lessons they have taught me—lessons that have required me to take real responsibility for my actions as an adult. And it hasn't always been fun.

My eldest had the unfortunate honor of being first. A lot of mistakes have been made in his short, eleven years of life. Ours is a roller coaster of a relationship. We have highs and we have lows. An early low that sent me back to therapy and to consultations with parenting experts took place when he was about a year old.

Skyler was speaking by the time he was eight months

and walking at ten months. His early development led me to wrongly assume he was emotionally intelligent enough to explain to me why he was often crying. On one particular day, I was alone with him when he began to cry for what, to me, seemed like no reason. I tried distracting him. I tried babying him. I tried the pacifier, food, diaper checks, etc. I tried asking him why he was crying. I tried ignoring him.

As each strategy got thwarted, my blood pressure rose, the tension mounted, and rage set in to the point that I screamed in a hurl of anger that must have looked like a monster roaring from his tiny vantage point: "What do you want from me?!" As the sound reverberated in my body and the room, I was instantly ashamed and my next memory was of the two of us on the floor crying with each other.

I had lost control. Being unable to control this human (nor my own time) helped me get in touch with some painful memories around feeling helpless. It was hard work recognizing and fighting the automatic trigger that feeling impotent to solve a problem or calm a situation made me feel. That incident triggered an opening for growth that I have not taken lightly. It was the beginning of recovering from being a control freak and the continued healing from my perfectionist tendencies.

He ministered to me by being the mirror to my lack of patience with myself. Unfortunately, it was manifested as impatience with him, but that's what therapy is for!

Learning to love Skyler wholly has defied every definition of what I thought a mother needs to be for her child. A wise friend said: "You want to love him like a blanket, but he needs you to love him like a tent." When I keep her words in the forefront, it works. He comes to me. He seeks me out. I am a safe space for him to find comfort, help, and fun.

I now dance between giving him his freedom and wanting to smother him, with love, that is. Skyler has an "it" factor that is amazing to observe. Since he was eighteen months old he was called the Mayor of Munchkin Land in his day care because all the children flocked to him. It's never changed. People still gravitate toward him, adults and kids alike. If I could bottle what he has, I would, but he doesn't even know he has it, so I doubt it's teachable.

Skyler has taught me a lot, and I live for the moments when we do connect and he remembers that he likes his mom. He does most things (boy things) with his dad, but sometimes when I am sitting on his bed keeping him company as he falls off to sleep, he gets super mushy and tells me he forgets how great I am and how much he loves me. When he lets me know I am not the horrible ogre I sometimes think I am, it's an incredible relief.

Each rough patch we hit has been another opportunity for growth, and oh, how I wish it were as easy as a game of Candy Land. But it's more like Monopoly—long and complicated with moments of great triumph. But thank goodness, we always return to love. Just like passing Go—we always get back to love.

So much dysfunction goes on around our behavior with our children, and although we'd like it to be different, we don't know where to look for the answers. I have learned that the people to look to are ourselves. Our children came here to be our teachers. They came to minister to our souls. If we find the lesson and work on it, we'll have fulfilled the contract mutually agreed upon by our two souls. The inner work they cause us to do may be the greatest meaning the relationship provides.

What does amuse me is how the same mother and father can reproduce and create distinct children. Here is mystery again. We would expect them all to be the same since the same elements are in place. For me, however, the relationship with each child is different, just like each child is. The love is the constant, but each has brought a different lesson, challenge, personality, and soul to work with me. As Skyler and I work it out, I also am in relationship with

Maya, his sister, three and a half years his junior and twin to her other brother, Wyatt.

Maya can be tougher than both boys put together, having endured more injuries and the first set of stitches among them. And yet she is all girl. She loves pink and purple and dresses and shoes and shopping and dance and all things creative. She was twin A and has an alpha dog personality. Although commandeering, she is graceful. She has a natural ability for ballet and dance that is astounding. She is creative. Kids like to play with her but my husband thinks that when it comes to him and me, she plays us. She is crafty and also verbally sharp. He sees a manipulator (his lesson to work through). She's also a big lover and giver. I see a smart girl who knows what she wants. I don't see her as manipulative.

For now, she seems to be bringing me the opportunity to celebrate the feminine and be softer and maternal—something that as an independent loner I can forget to do. She also presents me with the predicament of helping a strong-willed child become disciplined without losing her confidence and self-esteem. I am getting the chance through my only daughter to usher a female into womanhood and femininity. She has put me in touch with my own and I have been given the opportunity to shape how she sees herself and other women and how she will value herself in work, life, love, and all that awaits. It's a delicate dance to help her emerge as a strong female.

A couple of years ago, we took our kids to Disney World. The trip was two years in the making, and the kids were enlisted into saving jugs of change and putting on a garage sale to make it a family effort. Maya was particularly interested in the Princess Tea at Disney. It was an expensive treat to take her, my mother-in-law, and myself, but we were very excited and we had talked about it for months. The tea was a very feminine event, to say the least. Nothing, however, beat showing up to our appointed teatime only to find every girl except my daughter dressed head to toe in Disney princess gear. Some even wore wigs. All the favorites were represented, and I immediately felt the desperate social panic of showing up at an event improperly dressed. Miss Maya, as we often call her, was luckily (thanks to Grandma) dressed in a lovely garden dress with fancy shoes and an updo, but she's no dummy: she instantly caught the panic. The look of horror on her face was barely formed before we swooped her up and ran upstairs to the conveniently located Disney shop loaded with princess regalia.

We rummaged through the aisles and felt the frenzy mount, because as luck would have it, there was nothing in Maya's size. Here Grandma and I were, ready to plop down a couple of hundred dollars more to help Maya fit in, but truthfully, we were relieved when we all left empty-handed and ready to face our fate as the uncostumed lot.

Once the resolve was in place, Maya played the whole teatime fantasy with grace and poise. As it turned out, she was called on to stand next to the singing hostess to lead the group in a song. When she asked me if we could do our Fred Astaire–Ginger Rogers dancing as the piano player played, I shed any embarrassment and whirled her out in the middle of the floor, which was not even designated for dancing. Before we knew it, several other little girls had gathered around us and soon my mother-in-law and I were leading small groups of dancers with dozens of parents watching in either admiration or disdain (I could not tell which) at our ballsy-ness.

As inconsequential as the whole experience might have been, I came to see it as a perfect opportunity to help craft another "tomorrow's woman." Even though our knee-jerk reaction was to protect her from any pain by fitting in and joining the crowd at almost any cost, we were given the opportunity to rise above settling for the norm. We held our wigless and crownless heads up and had a great time.

Shaping a female whom you want so much for, and

whom at the same time want to shield from the pain of the mistakes you've made, means having to be really conscious of the messages you send her. She ministers to me by forcing me to be very conscious of the messages I give her, so therefore every thought I have. She watches when I don't eat dessert with everyone else and asks if I'm dieting. She overhears me lamenting my middle-aged body. She counts how often I leave home for business. I have to be of two minds as I lead my own life and monitor what I am teaching her about being a woman through it.

Of course, it's all in danger of being shot to hell when Maya pushes my buttons, which she does quite well, considering she is only eight. An extraordinarily defiant little human being, she tests my patience with her divine tenacity. And she cries about *everything*. Often my need for peace outweighs my capacity to be consistent with her. To help a spirited, strong-willed child remain powerful while teaching her kindness at the same time is no easy task. I have to work very hard to stay the course of the conscious parent. I recently discovered that the key with her is that she always needs to be right. So if I stop trying to be right as well, I can keep her defiance from escalating. I don't coddle her just to appease her, but I've learned not to fight to be right. If I allow her to be right in her point of view, even if it is not accurate, she will laugh at herself and stop her struggle. And lo and behold, I learn that I don't always have to be right either.

The path of remaining conscious with kids seems to hold the most reward and meaning. As hard as it is, I try to toe the line. My younger son, however, brings out my best more often than not.

Wyatt has epilepsy. He has visible seizures several times a day, sometimes a hundred a day. His brain scans show that he has seizures almost constantly. His seizures cause an involuntarily loss of control of his neck so that his head drops like a person dozing off. All of this affects his ability to keep up in school. He is cognitively all there but he needs the special help of his own personal aide in the classroom to help cement the basics that his first-grade classmates seem to just know by rote.

Wyatt's not as consistently verbal as his siblings, but I don't need the words to understand. I never have. By the time he was five months old, I knew something was up with Wyatt, because when he cried, there seemed to be no off switch. The same holds true now. He had no symptoms, however, until he was four, and even then it took catching him on video to prove to a doctor that I was not a nervous mother imagining that something was not as it should be. As I insisted on identifying the symptoms that only I could see, his ministering to me by just being in my life turned me into a crusader and someone who has had to challenge the experts whose expertise and training does not always allow them to see what my son needs.

Wyatt's brain has resisted every medication we've tried. And while every alternative method works temporarily, his brain reverts to the status quo. My stubborn boy has a stubborn brain. It does not want to budge out of its misfiring state.

He is a champion at blood tests and we have been hospitalized five times for EEG brain monitoring sessions over the last three and half years. We still have no answers as to where his seizures are originating in the brain, and the right treatment remains a guessing game. It has been incredibly frustrating, but knowing that it could be worse—that this is not a disease that will swallow him up completely as some other diseases might—consoles me. We take it day by day, trying very hard not to freak out, which feels like it would be easy to do. It's not that we don't think about it, but we try to stay in the present moment. But one day last summer, while we were on vacation, six-year-old Wyatt turned to my husband and me and said: "Is this epilepsy going to destroy my future?" He is extremely self-aware and deals with all of this with the maturity of someone six times his age. While some of his teachers have thought he is clueless, we know he is more clued in than he lets on. His wicked sense of humor shows us he gets what's going on.

Wyatt has a high emotional intelligence, which always reminds me that I can do better with my own. This child kisses me without me asking and holds my hand and tells me not to cry when they prod *him* with needles. He is quick to be polite and purposely infuriates his twin by behaving well when she is having a tantrum.

The wrenching part is that love is not enough to stop his brain from misfiring. I squeeze him tight wishing with all my might that I could suck the problem out of him. I hold his head between my hands and pray for the seizures to subside. I try to will it all away by focusing my glance on him intensely, as if I had superhero lasers beaming magical powers from my eyes. And yet what I know about prayer is that it's not supposed to be about asking for something to happen but rather to ask to be changed so that healing can occur. It's so easy to understand that as I pray for others. It is far harder when it's your child.

I don't want the strength to deal with it. I want it *gone*! But when I calm down, I can ask for the healing he has to do and the healing I have to do to understand the blessing of this challenge. Wyatt—what he brings me is the practice to find good where no one else sees it and to fight for what I see.

Children don't just come to us; they come for us. They come into our life and show us where our capacity to love can still use improvement. They shine a spotlight on our wounds and force us to deal with them. They minister to our soul's growth and our personal growth even if we don't like it. The alternative is to pass on the dis-ease, to leave them an inheritance that they'll have to sort out and try not to hand to the next generation. We have to let these small ministers do their very big work.

SEVEN

Manicures and Life Lessons

I'll never forget her voice. It was scratchy and frail and boisterous at the same time.

"Go away!" she yelled from underneath her sheets and blankets, a little bird seeking refuge in the corner of her nest.

"Go away!" she screamed, in a tone that matched pitch with a clarinet.

Olive was my assignment. I was twenty-five and not very sure of myself, but something told me not to obey her and go in the door of her tiny studio apartment on the Upper West Side of New York City. I was supposed to deliver food to her as part of my volunteer work. It was winter, and we were making sure elderly folks and shut-ins got food.

When I went inside, I could see a lump in the twin-size bed tucked in a corner of the room. It moved a bit as she yelled for me to go away one more time. As I quietly moved over the threadbare carpeting to get closer to the bed, she suddenly threw off her covers and screeched out one more command.

"Don't grow old! Now go away."

I told her I'd leave the food in case she got hungry, but before I left—God only knows where the idea came from—I turned back and asked her when was the last time she had had her nails done. I felt my throat tighten after I said it and tears started to fill my eyes. I was so scared. I asked if she had any nail polish and an emery board around.

What was I doing?

Olive sat up in her bed and leaned up against the wall. She was wearing pink two-piece pajamas—men's style, woman's fit—and she perked up just a bit as she pointed me toward a drawer and her manicure tools. Without words we both glided over to the small table and chairs just a couple of feet away from the bed that she seemed to hope would be her coffin.

As I massaged her hands and filed her nails, Olive's face changed before my eyes. It went from a grayish color to revealing a glint of pink in her skin. Her face transformed from tight and acrid to show the remnants of an attractive, sophisticated New York girl with amazing cheekbones and a strong jawline.

I don't remember too many words between us, but that day became the beginning of a biweekly manicure session with Olive. I came and did her nails and she told me about her glamorous life as a shopgirl at Bloomingdale's and how she made a terrible mistake never marrying or having kids. It was as if we were sent to each other. I kept her engaged in life for a few hours a month and she kept me from making the same decisions she had, which were already in danger of becoming permanent. My decisions to never marry or have kids were already ten years old, but she somehow managed to loosen them from the cement they were embedded in and make me question my resolve.

That summer, I had been away doing summer stock and missed a couple of my manicure days with Olive. When I showed up at her building one day, no one answered at her door. I felt a panic attack trying to set in (I had been having them for months), but I held it together and went to find the building manager in the lobby who sat behind the glass, in a cubby reinforced with iron bars.

"Where's Olive?" I said fearing his answer.

"They took her to Beth Israel," he said.

"When?" I asked, suddenly realizing it could be too late.

"Two weeks ago or something," he said, unconcerned.

I flew out of the building in a surreal waking dream. I got myself into a cab and to Beth Israel Hospital. I found Olive alive and completely out of her mind. She was strapped to the bed and screaming like crazy. I couldn't make out what she was trying to say. It was just screaming and moaning with an occasional "No!" thrown in.

This scenario was stretching me beyond my capacity as a twenty-five-year-old candidate for a nervous breakdown. I didn't know what to do with a screaming old lady I hardly knew. At least that was my first thought. But what I did was grab a rolling stool and move in close to her head. She had no idea who I was and didn't really see me anyway. Whoever she was yelling at was not visible or present (at least in flesh and bones). I leaned down to her ear and started whispering.

"It's okay, Olive. You don't have to fight anymore. Everything's fine. No one is going to hurt you."

She stopped screaming.

"You don't have to fight. There is nothing to be afraid of. You can rest now."

Olive took a deep breath and closed her eyes. I started to feel panicky again when I let the next words out of my mouth.

"You can go if you want to. It's okay. No more fighting. You can go."

"Oh my God!" I thought to myself. "Oh, please don't die in front of me. I don't think I can do that part!"

When I was sure she was asleep and not dead, I went out in the hall to find someone in charge. I didn't know how these things worked. Who was in charge of Olive? I found out that there was a social worker on her case and I left my number.

"Are you next of kin?" the nurse asked.

"No. I'm just a friend," I replied, feeling as if none of it was any of my business and questioning how I even got into the situation in the first place. As I took one more look into Olive's hospital room, I knew I wouldn't see her again. I was too afraid to come back and be there when she passed. All I could think of as I walked out of the hospital was the price of Olive's choices. I learned that the sacrifices it takes to let others into your life might be worth it. If Olive had made them she might have changed the end of her story. I knew I was open to changing mine.

There were four of us at Olive's funeral: the woman who held her power of attorney (she had worked with Olive at Bloomingdale's), the woman's husband, the clergyperson, and me.

I'll never forget Olive. What started out as a good deed changed my life.

There is no question in my mind that I was the one who received the most from the Laura–Olive cosmic matchup. I was supposed to be the giver—bringing food, manicures, and companionship—but she gave me my life. She turned my head in a different direction. It was a brief but intensely meaningful encounter. We connected at a critical time in each other's life. She improved mine and I'd like to think her passing was made the slightest bit easier. In some ways, she started me off as a minister more than a decade before it even occurred to me as a conscious thought.

In the Jewish tradition, giving back or doing a good deed is called a "mitzvah." The bar or bat mitzvah boy or girl at thirteen years of age does a community project as part of the requirements for completing this coming-of-age ritual. For when children do, they become a mitzvah—a blessing back to their community. The coming-of-age occurs when they are no longer just the beneficiaries of the blessings around them but also blessings, in the form of their giving back and taking responsibility for those they commune with.

Every religious tradition has a tithing, giving, and service component. We give to the contribution basket, write checks for projects, and put in our hours of volunteer work. It is part of how we have all been trained to be better citizens of the world. It brings meaning to our lives and makes us feel good. The undeniable truth that it makes us, the giver, feel good, brings up questions: Who wins when we perform a kindness? Who gains from giving? Who benefits from good deeds? Who is ministering to whom?

We all do. The intention is for the receiver to benefit but everyone gains. The goodness comes back. You may never see the money again or the coat you gave or the time you donated, but you will have gained something even though that's not what you set out to do. The Dalai Lama says that when we take care of others it is like taking care of ourselves, because we are all connected.

Fear is the biggest killer of mitzvah there is. We're afraid to get near the homeless person or talk to old people. They could be crazy and hurt us or they might smell terrible. We're afraid we won't have enough money if we give some away. We are afraid a gesture would not be big enough or good enough to matter. We are also afraid of intimacy or of getting sucked dry.

I know fear stops me from giving more of my time, my money, and myself. Mine comes in the form of being afraid that doing it once means I will have to keep doing it. People always come back for more and that terrifies me. I don't like to create a dependency that I then feel responsible for. I have enough people that depend on me to feed them or employ them. It's all I can handle. So, often, the instinct to give gets thwarted by my fear that I'll have added another person or organization to my cart that will now require a permanent seat. When I'm rational, I know that isn't true.

I'm reminded of a person I met, around the same time that I knew Olive, who never made me fearful that a kind gesture would become a burden I could not bear. He was a man who lived in my building on Twenty-third Street in Manhattan. I assume he was in his late fifties. He had salt-and-pepper hair, long limbs, and a tall build. He was completely crippled and bent over in a wheelchair. My guess is that he had cerebral palsy.

Frank loved to be outside, and every day his aide would roll him out onto the sidewalk in front of the building. Twenty-third Street is a very wide, busy, cross street in New York City. It was not a quiet side street and we were one hundred fifty yards from the corner of Seventh Avenue, another large, bustling street. This was a hub for rushed folks coming out of the subways and the commuter PATH train to walk to their offices on Sixth or Fifth Avenue.

There, in the midst of it all, was Frank—well groomed

and in a button-down shirt or handsome sweater, bobbing and weaving in his wheelchair, obviously excited about the commotion and activity right out in the middle of the sidewalk. He didn't like to sit to the side. He liked being in the middle of it like a kid standing in the ocean waiting for the waves to break on his body. His wide mouth would be hanging open and you could see his tongue flip-flopping in there like a fish on a dock after it's been freshly scooped out of the water. Needless to say, he did not get too many people to glance back at him. They would look beyond him and stay focused on their destination. Some would be annoyed that they had to navigate the obstacle he had created in their path. Others would see him from several feet away and dart across the sidewalk to avoid the slowdown that might ensue if they stayed on course.

I walked by Frank many times myself and for some unexplained reason, on one gorgeous, sunny day, I stopped to say hi. He got so excited I was afraid he'd slip out of his wheelchair. He bobbed and then closed his eyes to focus and try to talk. When the sounds started coming out, he opened his eyes and looked back up at me. He was very hard to understand but we did communicate. In short sentences, overpowered by how difficult it was to control his tongue, Frank would ask me questions about my life. He learned about my auditions and my waitressing job and my

workouts at the YMCA two doors down from our building. When I would try to find out more about him, he was
always cheery, but did not volunteer much. He wanted to
hear about me.

From that first day, I loved to take a few minutes to
talk to Frank when I saw him on the block. Except for
his aide, most people looked at us strangely as we laughed
and carried on. His flailing arms and bobbing head
always brought stares. But what a gem he was and how he
served me to keep my life in perspective and helped me
feel the privilege of always being greeted with excitement
by another human being. If I had stayed afraid, I would
not have had that wonder and connection. He ministered
to me and brought me into the awareness of being joyful.
I had to overcome my fear of him to do so.

One of the most interesting forms of fear and scarcity that I've seen in many guises over the years might
be expressed as: "If I can't do something big to change
the world, then I'm not going to do anything at all." I call
this phenomenon the "Mother Teresa syndrome." Individuals feel that they must have a Mother Teresa level of
accomplishment in their good deeds to make any difference, and when they realize they cannot, they do nothing. We'd rather do nothing. Scarcity is keeping it all to
yourself for fear that it is not good enough.

It's an easy trap to fall into. I understand. Heck, watching one *Oprah* show will make you feel like you ain't doing bubkes to make the world a better place. Talk about feeling inferior! But I will quote the mother herself to dispense the antidote. Mother Teresa said: "We do not do great things. We do small things with great love."

Mother Teresa did not wake up one morning and plot her greatness. She did not say: "Hey, if I pick up this one sick guy from the street and then get a bunch of nuns, ask them to wear tablecloths with blue stripes, pick up more sick people together, then surely, this will put me on the path to sainthood." She responded to what was right in front of her and did what she could do. One step at a time, she created something powerful but it was not a plan.

Voilà, the answer to our existential angst. Do small things with great love. Do Olive's nails, stop and connect with Frank, cut your neighbor's lawn, smile at everyone for a day—feel your world transform. Be the blessing. Be the mitzvah. Feel the meaning. Allow yourself to minister.

PART THREE

MAGNIFICENCE

If something has ever taken your breath away, you have been in the presence of magnificence. Whether it was a beautiful vista, a bride coming down the aisle, a work of art, or a child entering the world, true magnificence inspires a deep and enduring sense of awe.

Would it be too much to ask to feel this awe in our every-day lives? If we crave meaning, then we must, for magnificence and meaning are irrevocably intertwined. And the truth is that magnificence is actually easily available. Every day. Everywhere. It won't take much training to see it, but it does take willingness and openness and slowing down.

Before I went to seminary, I thought nothing of killing a

fly. Reading the many religious texts we studied, especially Buddhist writings, made me more aware of *every* sentient being. I could no longer absentmindedly crush these uninvited houseguests and I even encouraged my kids to follow my lead. I didn't realize that my then eight-year-old, Skyler, was already ahead of me on the value of the common housefly.

"Did you know that fly has four thousand eyes and can see in three hundred sixty degrees all at once?" he said.

"I've never really thought about it," I replied.

"Yeah, and every time it lands, it poops!" he went on.

"Wow, I never knew there was so much to a dirty fly," I said.

I saw a nuisance I was trying to learn to respect. Skyler saw magnificence. What's the difference between them? It isn't just the knowledge he collected from a science book or kid magazine, although knowledge can open the door to magnificence. It was a depth of seeing. I was looking at the matter on a surface level—he was looking deeper. And deeper is exactly where magnificence lies and where meaning can be found.

You can walk in the forest and see nothing, but if you pay attention you see a universe.

—Diane von Fürstenberg

~   ~   ~

All that is magnificent, find me now. May I experience majesty and take it in deeply. May that magnificence inspire me to be more. Help me see it and recognize it and embrace it so I may feel the fullness of contentment. From there, may I be able to share in a way that contributes to all sentient beings' having it too. May we all live from our own magnificence.

~   ~   ~

EIGHT

I Am Here to Be Seen

"I am here to be seen."
"I see you."
"I too am here to be seen."
"And I see you."

We spoke these words to each other during an exercise that the director of my seminary had paired us up to do. She had been inspired by the Zulu greeting *Sawubona*, a word that does not have a direct English equivalent. It translates loosely as "I am here to be seen." Aren't we all? Some claim they'd rather hide, but in truth, every human longs to be deeply seen for who they are. We long to be witnessed. "See me!"

Our relationships are the magnificent vehicles by

which we are seen and clearly they are one of the top three or four elements we equate with a meaningful life. We have friendships, families, work colleagues, lovers, spouses—all kinds of relationships.

A Course in Miracles warns against cultivating only special relationships and encourages readers to build holy relationships as well. Special relationships, the relationships we have with that special someone (romantic love) and those closest to us (family and friends), are called special because we tend to reserve our love and most generous spirit for those who are dearest to us, those who are special to us. Yet this generosity should not be reserved for only the "special" people in our life. If more meaning in our life is what we are looking for, we must aim to make it available to all.

How is it possible to build and maintain a holy relationship with everyone we encounter? Sometimes when we fall in love romantically, we see so deeply into the other person's being that it is possible to find love in our heart for them no matter who they are and what they've done. The same is true for the love we have for our children. If we say we want more meaning in our life, we need to be awakened to the opportunity to experience this kind of love for anyone anywhere. Those we work with, those we interact with in our daily chores—be it at the grocery store, the mall, or the bus stop—there are around us at any given time countless people who deserve to be in a holy relationship with us. To see the divine, the good, the right, the tender, blessed child in every person. That is a holy relationship. That is magnificence.

One of the blessings from the yoga and Hindu traditions that I love best is *Namaste*. The Sanskrit word literally means "I bow to you," and the saying of it is to be accompanied by a subtle gesture—you place your hands in front of your heart in a prayer position and bow slightly to the other person. The bow shows reverence. The greeting has come to mean "The divine in me greets [or meets] the divine in you."

The Yoruba tradition uses the term *ashe* to mean the essential divine nature in everything. It is the ideal that within all things lives sacredness if looked for with "deep seeing eyes."[1] Even negative people or events are not void of *ashe*; it just takes deeper eyes to see it. With deep seeing comes deep feeling, connection, and meaning. Having this ability to see deeply brings us to a miraculous oneness. Seeing deeply is the purpose of any relationship,

[1]From Huston Smith, *World Religions* (San Francisco: HarperSanFrancisco, 1991).

whether it began as special or not. I know firsthand that this can be so much easier said than done.

Usually, I find it easy to find the divine in strangers I meet along my path. It may be on an airplane, at the mall, on a campground—just anywhere. I find it easy to connect with them, usually being the one who starts the conversation especially if I see them looking awkward wondering if they should say something. I can find something in them across any cultural, racial, or physical boundaries to connect with them on. As my eyes meet theirs and a smile warms my face, it's almost as if my upturned expression turns on a faucet that empties love into my heart. Much more difficult is finding the divine in those who test my patience and goodwill.

When I lived in my studio on Twenty-third Street in New York City, I had a neighbor who was very elusive. Our apartments were separated only by an elevator shaft, yet we never spoke to each other. She would rush into her apartment and close the door to avoid eye contact with me, and she often left things that got in my way in the narrow hallway. She was a chubby woman in her forties, with big blue eyes and curly chestnut hair, who always seemed distracted, in a rush, and somewhat messy and eccentric. I had some animosity toward her only because at the time it was hard not to take it personally that she never looked up to say hello. I didn't hate her, but I just never gave any thought to her behavior other then being annoyed by it.

One winter in particular, I happened to casually notice that the hats or head scarves my neighbor usually wore no longer had chestnut curls falling from them. There was no evidence of her head being shaved, her hair had clearly fallen out.

"Oh my God," I remember thinking. "She's got cancer!"

After I made that discovery, the opportunity to run into her had not come up until one night, when I went to throw the trash into the incinerator. I found her sitting in the stairwell smoking a cigarette.

"I've never seen you smoke," I said.

"It's not a good time to start," she said. "I wanted to keep the smoke out of the apartment. You know, I am really sorry for all the stuff I leave in the hallway sometimes. I had to lose a breast to figure out it was time to let go of some of the stuff in my apartment."

I didn't know how to react at first.

"You don't have to apologize." I could feel shame washing over me as I realized I had known nothing of this woman's pain.

"I noticed you had lost your hair, but I had no idea you had cancer. I'm so sorry."

"It's okay," she said. "I am going to be all right. But I am learning so much and I know this happened to me because I can't let go of anything. I can't let you in to see, but my apartment is floor-to-ceiling shoes, furniture, newspapers, and boxes, with a few little pathways to walk through. I know I have to clear this place out."

I don't remember how the conversation ended that night, but I do remember that we went on to be friendly to each other. We found that we shared a religious upbringing and a love of vintage shoes and all things bohemian. She moved away a couple of years later, and while we never became close enough that we might have kept in touch, her presence had taught me so much. Through the realization that her earlier behavior had had absolutely nothing to do with me, I learned that taking personally such small things as a failure to say hello was a waste of energy. If I had known to see more and look more deeply, I may have recognized her magnificence sooner. She was a sweet person with a tough life. I felt so bad for having ever been annoyed with her. If I had asked about the stuff in the hall, I might have learned about her living conditions earlier and maybe could have helped her. Her perfection was a given, but I never bothered to look.

And there are lessons too within romantic relationships. Falling in love is pretty easy. Sex is easy. Love is harder. And staying in love is even harder still. There is that obvious rush of emotion and excitement from a new relationship that can make you punch drunk, but the real invitation is to enter a vessel for shared growth. Approaching it consciously, every relationship is an opportunity for awareness and transformation.

My own relationship carried its own one-two punch of early headiness followed by sobering growth. If a "special relationship" begins with being punctured by one of Cupid's infamous arrows, then my relationship with my husband is indeed a special one. When I first laid eyes on Mark, I felt a surge of energy run through me. It wasn't head to toe, it was more horizontally, as if it cut right through me. It was quick. If it had occurred in a movie, the movie would have been *The Matrix*. I have an image of myself being momentarily taken by the same energy that hit Keanu Reeves in this film, hair flying back, arms involuntarily whooshing behind me.

I was standing in the lobby of the Dupont Hotel in Delaware where one of my best friends was marrying one of Mark's best friends. It was stately and elegant, marble floors and ceilings, chandeliers and regal staircases. I was at the bottom of the wide staircase that fanned out where I stood when Mark rushed into the lobby just above. He was carrying his guitar case and his luggage and he was in a rush being the last groomsman to arrive. We were already taking pictures before the ceremony. I caught one glimpse of him: long, dark hair in a ponytail, beard, big brown eyes, beatniky, artsy-fartsy-looking, his strong arms wrapped around his belongings and barely covered by his cutoff T-shirt. In the split second when I took all this in, I felt that Cupid-arrow energy. Before I could register it, he had disappeared into the elevator.

His next entrance was in his tux, all cleaned up and look- ing very handsome. There was no second Cupid's arrow, but I was giddy and uncharacteristically flirtatious as I pinned his corsage on and filled him in on the rehearsal he had missed the night before. We had been paired up in the wedding party. (Our friends take credit for our union, to this day.) He later told me that he thought: "Gee, she must be one of the bride's peppy musical theater friends." He also thought I seemed an easy target. He had no idea what a loaded gun he was playing with.

Anyway, I could not keep my eyes off him for the entire ceremony as we stood under the chuppah while my Jewish friend married his Lebanese-American Christian friend. He was handsome—no, dashing—and I wondered what he was thinking during the ceremony. At the reception, we danced like we'd known each other our whole lives and the deal was sealed by the time the bridal party hung around after the wedding and Mark entertained with his guitar. I was smitten. And so was he. He taught himself guitar in high school just to have girls cave in to its charm, and it worked. We have been together ever since.

It was by no means a straight shot to happily-ever-after. Finally being seen deeply and loved anyway was part of the meltdown I talked about earlier in this book.

Mark had work to do on himself too. It took us three years from love at first sight to a wedding, but the growth we each had to go through to get there made our eventual ceremony a fabulous reward. The specialness of the start was the powerful draw that took us to the mat individually and collectively. We've been in and out of holy and special for more than eighteen years.

The strongest relationships in our lives are like holy vessels (it is called a relation*ship*, after all!) that shine light on our ability to expand and develop a greater capacity for love. And this doesn't necessarily mean just better sex and mutual pampering but rather to find the ability to see the good, even in the unpopular moments of anguish or stubbornness or blindness or ignorance—and to transfer that love and patience to everyone we meet. Learning to love also means learning to crack open the parts of ourselves that we need to care for. This is often where some of the hard work to be done is, but the reward can be great.

In a truly holy relationship, the decision to keep loving is renewed and reaffirmed over and over again. If all we want to do is to change someone else day in and day out, we are not loving them. If we are in constant tension and battle, no matter how much we love each other, we are not loving each other well. As a wise, old bartender once said to me when I was struggling with the decision to get married, "Do you bring out the best in each other or do you bring out the worst in each other?" We come together to grow. To love often means loving each other into positive change. And in some cases, that change involves parting ways.

In the last five years I have been called on to usher several women through stages of infidelity in their marriages. In every case, it was the women doing or considering the cheating. It was a privilege to be trusted with their most intimate feelings during these times, but it was also a personal challenge to keep my focus on where the love was—to push any judging feelings I might have about infidelity aside and stay focused on what their hearts were crying for. Maybe their marriage was something worth fighting for? Or maybe they really had found a new, more meaningful love—a love that was meant to be? In the end, I was there for all of them without judgment. Championing love put me on the other side of the fence from where judgment would have placed me. Judgment would have put me in the role of telling them they were wrong. Instead, I tried to see them deeply as whole, perfect people who were suffering. And I came to see that they had been (or were) tempted to cheat because they had lost the connection to their spouses that made their relationship meaningful. They were looking for meaning—something that might give them the feeling of being connected to another person or themselves.

To help them straddle the line between the promises they had broken and the desire to be loved and seen for who they were was very difficult. Keeping my focus on their search for the magnificent fuel that love is allowed me to stay in the conversation with them. I wanted them all to regain happiness and I could not judge how that would come to pass. In other words, I could not tell them to stay or to go.

One particular woman who eventually got divorced had suffered for years because her spouse did not cherish her. He was too wrapped up in his own problems and she rarely felt like she was there, much less loved, adored, and seen deeply for who she was. She spent her whole marriage doing the work for both of them to keep the marriage going. Exhausted, but willing to keep working on her marriage, she found herself in a collegial relationship that started to find roots outside the appropriate boundaries. She began to recognize all that was missing in her primary relationship.

As it turns out, she married the new man, and he adores her and lets her know it all the time. Even with her newfound happiness, she spoke of how hard it was to accept that the step to continue the holy relationship between she and her first husband—the step that would allow for the most growth and continued love—was to split. She wanted it to work. She wanted to keep her family together. She finally had to admit that their vessel/relationship had to change form for either of them to continue to grow. That form was to become friends after divorce, which they are as they raise their kids together but apart, with grace. It required her mourning the romantic love story that brought them together and seeing him more deeply as the man she shared a life with and without whom she'd not have her children. Despite his mistakes and flaws, she greeted the divine in him and he in her as the new form their relationship took played out.

It's so easy to be bitter. The smallest things can build huge walls of separation when cemented by resentments. Old hurts felt again and again make it hard to forgive. The significance in a relationship is not the attachment to the pain or the wrong that we feel was committed against us. The meaning comes from healing the separation. That goes for the separation between intimates and strangers alike. It doesn't always mean making up, having renewed togetherness or making a new friend, but it does mean fueling the vessel—the space between us that is our relationship—close or distant—with love so that peace can be ours. Without it, we keep ingesting poison (hate, resentment, anger) despite the physical distance we keep from our antagonist. When we can release the bitterness and get back to love, the freedom invites magnificence again.

Magnificent is the healing power of love and the synergy of what two people can produce when there is *namaste*—whether it's a family, a business, a good deed, a mutual growth spurt, something mystical, or something material. It is not likely to happen alone. Some of the best things we get to do as humans, like create another life, cannot happen alone. We often think better and produce more in a relationship with certain others than we do on our own. When we recognize this, we see that we have meaningful exchanges on our hands. What is magnificent is our desire to make our relationships work. What we fight for, what we might endure, what we hope for and what we are able to forgive. Whether it's continuing to champion your child when they are making bad choices for their life or making slow progress understanding a sibling so you can continue to be in favor with each other, we persevere and champion the love. That is the miracle.

I get that it is not easy. Seeing the divine in my husband and feeling the magnificence is challenging, to say the least, when he forgets to give Wyatt his medication or when the twins ate red pepper flakes on his watch. There is no *namaste* when he wants to have sex and I want to sleep because I have been up three nights in a row with a sick kid or when I get pulled over by cops for an expired registration on his car when the new one has been hidden on his desk for two years. My beloved gets his head chewed off and my children get to see "mean Mommy," as we call her, when they are all the most precious blessings in my life. But they see the real me as I see the real them beyond our idiosyncrasies and dramas.

The magnificence of love can hold the crazy moments. It can endure those moments of temporary blindness when we cannot see what's right. It is the glue that holds the vessel together so we can kick and scream as we grow and still be seen for who we truly are. Within that safe space, we evolve. The gratitude we feel for the safety of being seen is our path to meaning.

NINE

Being Special

We are, all of us, intent on laying claim to some piece of this world. We long to appear distinct from everyone else—and for some it doesn't seem to matter *how*, be it that they're coveted, aggrandized, victimized, or marginalized. All of us want to stand apart, but the funny thing is that quite often being special is about being the same. We have been mistaken in thinking that meaning can be derived from holding some special distinction. Our search for meaning is better served by looking at our sameness—that core part of all of us that is human. This is where our true magnificence and meaning lies. As humans, we have resilience, creativity, compassion, love, innovation, ingenuity, faith, reasoning, language, and pain transformed to good deeds. We share the magnificent miracle of life. Yet it takes great courage to reconcile that we are just part of the human family. We are nothing special *and* truly magnificent at the same time.

By the same token, we sometimes cling to our sameness to the detriment of seeing this human potential. In our effort to hold on to our way (or that of our family, race, religion, or tribe) we insulate ourselves, never turning to observe the lives of others around us who are different. We confine ourselves to what is familiar, when we could enhance our life by opening ourselves up to the richness that other cultures and ethnic groups have to offer. There is magnificence in what is strange or unfamiliar to us. It is only fear that holds us back from recognizing it and being enriched by it.

I understand that it's just easier to be with your own kind. There is less explaining to do. There is more comfort. But does meaning come from comfort or does it come from exploration, learning, and bleeding past the borders of the social constructs we've created?

I am not big on holding on to regrets, but I often wonder what would have been different in my own life if I had reached beyond the borders of race when I was younger. While I was on my way to earning my union status as a stage actor, I worked at a theater in Philadelphia. On my breaks, I would wander the neighborhood, browsing in stores that grabbed my interest. One time, I stopped into an art-supply store and a very handsome young African-American man asked if he could help me find something. I never intended to buy anything, but letting him help me led to flirting and a date to have coffee the next day.

I was pretty inexperienced about dating. Long-term boyfriends I had had, but meeting strangers and making a date was a different, new happening. I showed up the next day right on time, and coffee became dinner, and dinner became a romantic walk home that ended at the front door to my apartment high-rise with a nervous peck on the cheek and a quick fleeing upstairs.

The next day, my parents happened to be in town for a visit, and over dinner, I thought I'd give my new venture of going out on a date with a dark-skinned man a whirl.

"I went out with the most beautiful black man last night," I said.

"You *what*?" they shrieked in unison.

They freaked; I backpedaled. I said I was only joking, claiming that I said it only to see how they'd react.

I stood up the guy the next day when we were supposed to meet for lunch. I did not have the experience and fortitude to follow the wonder of meeting a warm, new friend because my parents would not understand if I strayed from my "own kind." I am ashamed to this day and have earmarked this as one of the things I'd go back and change if I had a time machine. What did I have to lose by trying? What did I have to gain by being afraid?

The benefit of giving up membership in our own predictable tribe is an expanded capacity for love. Ultimately, we all seek love. That is our collective connection. Some of us give it and some of us are still looking for it. Some of us have given up trying or go after it in ways that make us seem unlovable. Ultimately, it seems our quest to be special is just our struggle to feel whole, loved, and no longer afraid. It's our plea to feel magnanimous. But the more special and precious we become, the harder it is to be whole because we have forged separation between our true self and other people.

Giving up being special and separate is not that easy. It can become an identity and a way of life.

A couple of years ago, I was having dinner while on business in Florida with a seminary friend, Jackee, who has a huge presence. She is a black woman who can lead a prayer like no one I've ever seen. She can move a room with the fervent passion she exudes when she is channeling prayer and God's word. She is also pissed as hell.

We were at dinner in a nice restaurant, and the conversation got around to what I did for a living. We were still getting to know each other, since our class time did not allow for a lot of visiting. We were polite, but Jackee was gently pressing me about why anyone would ever need to hire a personal coach, why there aren't many black coaches, and for that matter, why there aren't more black people hiring coaches. I had some observations to share with her about cultural differences and family structures and trust, blah, blah, blah, when Jackee blurted out impatiently:

"Do you *have* any black friends?"

"Yes." I said, not liking where the conversation was headed.

"No. I mean like come-to-your-house-for-dinner black friends?" she said.

"Yes!" I said with annoyance as Jackee tilted her head and pursed her lips, raising her eyebrows like a mom suspecting her teenager of lying.

I was being a hundred percent truthful, so I was not about to start defending myself. However, as it set in that I was being tested and that Jackee and I had not bonded at the level I thought we had, I grew disappointed. She did not trust me. I could see that the wall she had put up was too high for me to climb. There were no words that would close the gap. It was going to take time if the circumstances would allow it. Really, it should not have surprised me if I had picked up on earlier hints that feeling separate was a heavy part of Jackee's experience.

A few months earlier, at a famous Jewish deli in Manhattan during a lunch break from class, Jackee and Ayleen, another classmate, were telling me about some of their humiliating experiences as women of color. Jackee has too often endured being followed into dressing rooms when she goes shopping with her daughter, because shopkeepers assume they are stealing. Ayleen spoke of how she is often mistaken for the doorperson at the federal government office where she works. I was sickened by what they were telling me. But then they let me in on something that, as a stupid white girl, I was not clued into and that made me feel even worse. Apparently, the black community is divided more deeply than I knew. I had been privy to the disdain between very light-skinned blacks and darker blacks, but I did not realize that there were more inside divisions, like yellow-black, blue-black, and high-red black.

Here we are, in a world where black people do not want to be judged by the color of their skin, and yet it's likely that within the community itself, that color will be pointed out with great importance. How can separation exist on this level together with the expectation of healing the divide in ourselves and our groups? Jackee's and Ayleen's stories, and the conundrum that came out of them, sat with me like the heavy potato knish I was picking at during lunch. I felt as if I had been punched hard in the stomach. I could understand how easy it is to grasp at specialness as a justified reason not to trust but rather to isolate and separate.

Other groups build walls within their own larger group too. If you're a Reform Jew, you're not Jewish enough to the Conservatives, and certainly not to the Orthodox. If you're Euro-Asian, you're not really Asian. If you are not credentialed or don't have a Ph.D. and don't hang out with academics, then you are "less than." If you are not a pure-bred, then you must be a second-class mutt.

I find it very disturbing when couples who might be willing to adopt a child can't or are persuaded not to because they are of a different race from the child's. Is it really better for a child to be raised in a culturally compatible home even if that means going longer without love and attention? Is it fair to keep a child from a loving home if it is to have same-sexed parents? Love is love. Isn't that where the meaning comes from?

I can't help wondering as I hear people grumble about the world being so different today—so many blended races and families—if it is not really just part of some divine plan to see our world become smaller and less divided. Those who long for the good old days when races didn't mix or neighborhoods were more segregated by religion or culture are really saying they need to feel safe by way of specialness. I can relate to that safety and how it is unsettling to lose it, but we also have to weigh the cost of keeping it.

When I was not quite six years old, my parents moved our family to Caracas, Venezuela. Within weeks of arriving, I spoke the language fluently, and no one believed I was a transplanted American. *"¡Esta niña es caraqueña!"* they would say. (This girl is from Caracas, born and bred!)

I had always loved that specialness. Speaking Spanish with a Venezuelan accent, considering my comfort foods rice and beans and fried plantains and feeling an affinity for the Latin people are gifts that were reaped from that time in a new land. I can still tap into the feelings of wonder as I saw huge mountains around the valley of Caracas and relishing how different life was there. Even our house was different. Nothing was made of wood. Concrete and stone kept the houses cool from the heat of the equator. Every home included maid's quarters. Every window was shrouded with iron bars to protect people from the deep social divide of haves and have-nots. In fact, the abbreviated description I used for years to describe my years there is: "On Sunday the maid went home, we didn't make our beds, and we went out to dinner." That was my life—one I thought was good.

The Latin music, the slower speed of life, and the tight-knit community did not follow me back to the States. What got left behind was a richness that celebrated the joy of being alive. There was not the same pressure there in sixth grade that there was here. There was no stress about fitting in and wearing the right clothes and showering with the proper frequency. In Venezuela, for the most part, I could bask in the warmth of a people who valued family and connectedness and relished being alive.

When I was acting in New York City, one of my agents tried to get me into auditions for Spanish-language commercials. There were not as many Hispanic actors then as there are now, so there was room for a white girl who could fake it. However, seeing myself among a room of predominantly Latin people in a New York City casting office was the first time it really hit me that I was not Latina. My skin was whiter than everyone else's. My eyes were not as deeply dark. My hair betrayed me too. I suddenly felt like an impostor.

Intellectually, of course, I had known I was not Latina, but until that day I didn't own in my heart that I wasn't really one. It was such a loss to me. I had to give up some specialness. The sadness eventually melted into nostalgia and now takes on the form of an open heart. I'll always have an affinity with Latin people. I have a ticket to connection, and I cherish it.

Who knows whether we'll ever be one, big, happy world where we all get along. Perhaps it's not possible. But the truth is we can move a whole lot closer together if we learn to connect on the level of being human, the one commonality we all have. We may never fully understand one another's suffering, but we do know suffering, so we have a common understanding. We may not have one another's problems, but we all have problems. We may not have the same ailments, but we know what pain is like.

If we could accept one another's efforts to understand as genuine, we could connect. If we give up being attached to our pain, our differences, our heritage, our history, and our specialness we can stop securing the abyss of our differences and score the meaning we crave.

TEN

Oh My God!

"Oh my God!"

From the devout to the agnostic, the phrase "Oh my God!" stands in our lexicon as a testament to all that is incredible, from the good to the catastrophic. It's also often a throwaway line. In fact, most people who use the phrase aren't really addressing God; they are just using an everyday expression.

I tease my mother-in-law, a firm atheist who wishes she could provide herself the comfort that believers have, relentlessly. She does not believe in God, yet her favorite phrase is "Oh my God!" (in a healthy Long Island accent).

I find it amusing that the word "God" can mean so much and so little. Something so magnificent to so many is just a figure of speech to others. What is not amusing at all, and in fact hurts to think about, is the irony of that magnificence being the cause of so much pain in the world because of semantics or varying interpretations. And yet, if there is a common source of meaning that many human beings have found, it is God. The belief in God or a higher being (or whatever you want to call him, her, or it) has defined our lives for thousands of years.

Karen Armstrong, noted religious commentator, says: "Throughout history, men and women have experienced a dimension of the spirit that seems to transcend the mundane world." And, she notes, the meaning of God has changed with the needs of man.

Early civilizations could not explain rain and thunder and all the magnificence of nature, so they called them the work of gods. These archetypal figures provided them with the feeling that they were protected. They also incited fear in these believers—the fear that if they didn't behave a certain way there would be dire consequences. Eventually, some civilizations condensed their belief into one God. One who made all and knew all. The Old Testament describes a vengeful God, one that I've heard the Reverend Michael Beckwith call the God "who seriously needed anger management." The New Testament brought a more benevolent God. Yet Christianity and Judaism were not the only ones laying claim to their creator. We have Islam, Sufism, Hinduism, and many, many more ways that humans see as the bricks that hold their lives in place. We have an overwhelming need to answer that which may be unanswerable, but boy, do we try.

I was set on a typical path of being born into my family's religion. I didn't always hate going to synagogue as a kid—that came later. When I was very young, around five, I can remember walking with my dad to shul (which I didn't think much of, other than that it had a funny name) and being so happy to have him to myself. I have no memory of the service, just the special time with my father.

By my tween years, it became harder and harder for me to go to religious services. It felt hypocritical to attend synagogue only twice a year for the most religious Jewish holidays. I did not connect with the prayers or the language used in the prayer books. I never had a rabbi who stirred my soul or my thinking. It felt like a penance to have to attend anything at the temple. It may have just been teenage angst and ambivalence, but I really think it was more. I wasn't finding meaning.

By the time I was sixteen, one particular sermon ended my participation in any organized religion for a great long while. I still have the image vividly available to me of the rabbi leaning over the pulpit—white-knuckling both sides of it with his aging hands. He jutted his face out to the audience, squinting his eyes closed behind his Coke-bottle glasses, and said: "You don't do good deeds because you are a good person. You do good deeds because you are a good Jew."

"That's it! I'm outta here!" I thought. I felt physically tethered to my seat in agony, as I awaited the service to be over. I never "bought in" again.

That began a spiritual quest that continues to this day. I no longer blame Judaism for my earlier disdain of organized religions, but it was those early experiences that made me realize that all the religions claim the same virtues to be their own and claim their path as the ultimate one to God. The "My dog's better than yours" club of organized religion just did not make sense to me. I realized you could be a very spiritual person and not be religious or tethered to any one tradition. It's always felt more meaningful *not* to be part of any one religion but to be free to connect to any of those that appealed to me.

Where today I appreciate the sweet traditions of Judaism, I am also an equal-opportunity God person. I can relate to Jesus, Mohammed, the Buddha, Olorun of Yoruba tradition, the "unknowable source of all things" and many more. Most of the time, I just live in the space where God is simply goodness. We are goodness. All that is good is God. All that is good, even when it comes with tragedy or upset, is God. In fact, I have an acronym for God: G-O-D. Goodness-Out-Dhere (I was born in Brooklyn, thus the accent on "there"). Goodness out dhere and in here, my heart. That is God.

Good is the moment when you taste something that sends your whole body reeling. Good is a precious moment when a child loves you with their eyes and you feel a flash of understanding of what life is about. Good is a kiss—from a peck on the cheek from someone you really care about to an electric, knee-weakening one from a lover. Good is feeling grounded in possibility and believing in your own abilities. Good is everything that grows and lives and breathes and plays a role in the sustainability of you. Is that not magnificence?

For a lot of people, my definition of God is considered too wishy-washy, especially for those who have the option of putting "Reverend" in front of their name. Having given sermons from a pulpit, I have been challenged by those who feel I don't believe in God the way they do. The truth is, I go in and out of experiencing God as a single, personal entity available to my every prayer.

On some days, there is a personal God. The one I have a relationship with when I lie down for shevasana (final resting pose) in yoga class or sit down to meditate, whom I ask to feel, to know, to embrace, to walk like in the world.

I go to bed every night thanking God for the day that has just passed and for the fact that all those I love are with me and intact. I wake up every day and ask to know God. I don't mean developing a better relationship with the *being* we call God, but more in the sense of me being more adept at walking through the world as someone who can see everyone as God would see them—divine creations. As I intensely focus on willing a cure for my son's epilepsy, I hear myself praying: "God, please help us." "God, please take his seizures away." "God, please let us learn what we are supposed to learn from this so we can move on." The personal God helps me draw from a source greater than what I can provide in that moment. And then there is the other side, which does not embrace God as a personal friend, guide, or mother/father.

My G-O-D operating system is God too, but it is not a one-on-one experience; it is an extension of oneself evidenced in all that exists. It is a connection to all things. My existence is evidenced in all that is and vice versa. The magnificence of everything becomes my fuel and my magnificence is part of "it." To me, that is a huge playground, which I believe gives the greatest opportunity for meaning. It is readily available and requires no dogma or specific regime to follow. Every thing and every One is a conduit to a meaningful connection.

The fact that I function from two different definitions of God is not unique. Questioning and changing our minds about God is part of the process. I'm sure I was not the only person surprised by the recent release of Mother Teresa's letters and diaries divulging that she suffered from a crisis of faith for decades. One of Christianity's greatest modern icons doubted the presence of God and his guidance. She persevered for half a century with a gnawing darkness in her consciousness, but still doing the work she believed was her partnership and service to a God she doubted. It's only natural to experiment with what is true for you. Everyone questions. It's one of the primary ways we create meaning as we draw the inexplicable magnificence toward us. It's part of the experience of being alive.

Whether we experience God or not, whether we have a formal faith or not, an organized belief system brings meaning to our life. When we can explain the magnificence of our existence and of nature, we're more at ease and satisfied. Even if we can't understand all things, if we feel connected to ourselves and to others, especially those that share our beliefs, we find meaning.

Where we go wrong is in believing one way of experiencing God exists to the exclusion of all others. War, genocide, division, and hatred are the opposite of goodness. Yet they are the result of defending what so many believe to be G-O-D.

We need only look at nature to see that we are still tethered to our most primal instincts. Just as animals fight for the survival of the fittest, so do we fight for our beliefs and religions. We fool ourselves into thinking that if we can kill off the others we will remain the dominant ones. Is that really what religion is for?

Part of the issue, I think, is that many religions demand that their followers live modern lives according to a set of doctrines thousands of years old. Yes, there are fundamental truths to be found in them, but we must take great care not to follow outdated truths about how life works. Surely, studying the past helps us avoid mistakes in the future, but when we operate via texts that are ancient, we have to make modern concessions. We update our textbooks in schools to reflect new knowledge, but religions are much slower in giving up tradition. Dietary laws in Judaism (keeping kosher), for example, were created out of health concerns for unrefrigerated stores of food. We have refrigerators, so why keep kosher? Clearly, it's tradition. It also involves rules about more humane treatment of animals that are slaughtered, which is a consciousness we still appreciate today. Its custom, however, illustrates dutiful devotion to one's interpretation of God's laws, and there are the more modern Conservative and Reform versions that don't require it. Keeping kosher is a simple example. There are bigger issues, but the point is that many faiths follow doctrines that were created for a world that works very differently from our own. We have modernized. Few faith traditions have.

As a people and a global culture, we have evolved technologically and physically (we live longer), but where is the evolution of the consciousness that honors magnificence? Certainly, there is evidence of some: most societies today no longer beat children into submission as a form of discipline. We have sexual harassment laws and, among other things, are humanizing the workplace and caring about renewable resources and green living. We are, however, fooling ourselves if we believe that crimes against humanity based on religious bias happen only elsewhere. *War* and *genocide* are big, scary words, but they can also be apt for smaller situations. Hating your neighbors or judging the person who does not share your value system—these small individual acts are the fuel that can feed larger human atrocities. What people forget is that many of the uglier ideas in our world (the ideologies of the Ku Klux Klan, the Nazi Party, Al-Qaeda, for example) are fed by smaller, more intimate kitchen-table discussions. And while conflict around God may appear to be the crux of the problem—God himself (or herself) has been effectively snuffed out.

One of the greater challenges for those who wish to engage in a meaningful exchange with God or spirit is in understanding how evil can exist in the face of a greater good that stands at the core of our collective belief system. How can terrorists commit those acts? How can Osama bin Laden plan the demise of U.S. citizens and then act upon his plan? One of my friends asked me this very question not long ago.

My answer is twofold. First, the question is about the bigger picture. Why does evil exist at all? As there is duality in every person, there is duality in the world. It's almost as if we need evil, for without it how would we know good? Without darkness, how do we recognize light? Darkness is an invitation to all of us to turn on the light. We are reminded in the presence of evil to light our own light so that we can let goodness take the lead.

Second, we must consider the individual we say is evil. When someone is working out of the evil side of his nature, he often doesn't believe that he is evil.

As an actor, I studied human motivation. If I were to play an evil character, my character would have to have a motivation that makes their evil the right thing to act on.

Villains feel justified. Their mental construct of the situation makes them right. Terrorists believe that they are acting in the name of God and, therefore, that their actions are actually holy and will be rewarded in heaven. The interpretation of the scripture that guides them is misinterpreted in the eyes of the rest of us, but the wrong-doer has found a way to make it dignified and the correct way to act. So when someone says to me, "How can God allow something like that?" I have to answer that even if you believe in an all-knowing God, the human condition still allows us free will. And free will allows many acts against humanity. And as we well know, terrorists are not the only villains on today's world stage.

Sometimes, even we are evil. We snuff out our own magnificence. How can God allow us to eat that extra piece of cake? Or smoke another pack? Or hit our kid? In those moments, we are so far away from magnificence. We have free will and we find a way to justify our "less than" side to gain some perceived reward, even if it is only a temporary one. The invitation then becomes to stay conscious and take our wounds out of the darkness so we can create something good from them. In the pain that maims lies an opportunity to heal separation, create meaning, and find a footing in a behavior that allows us to be fully available to ourselves and others.

During my seminary course, as we covered religion after religion, my ability to hold on to one way of seeing the world, and seeing God (or not) was dissolving and looking for a new form. In being open to all, I could not stay married to one. I was comfortable with that, but as I discussed God with one of my colleagues who is a fervent believer, I could not defend any one viewpoint. That frustrated me, but then I had barely a point of view. I was feeling a little lost, but not unhappy. I knew that what I was studying was causing a transition in me and that I'd land in a new place soon.

On that particular day, my fellow student Erika and I were continuing our discussion during our lunch break while walking along Ninth Avenue in New York City during its annual International Food Festival. The avenue was closed to traffic, and every inch was filled with booths offering foods from all over the world. We stopped at a Thai booth since I was craving some sweet pad thai for lunch. I took one bite of the warm and tasty dish. Comfort and pleasure made my shoulders come up to my ears and a sigh come out of my mouth. I was overcome by a wonderfully warm feeling and a bolt of clarity hit me.

"This is how I experience God," I said.

Erika laughed, and under her breath said: "Oh my God."

I enjoyed her appalled reaction and thought to myself: "No wonder Jews eat so much."

PART FOUR

MIND

No more powerful weapon do we wield against ourselves than the power of our own minds. When used to destroy, the mind is dangerous. It is like a potent drug—so well trained at addicting us to our own negativity and creating tapestries of false truth that can be difficult to unravel. The negative thought pattern can become so well worn in the brain that the slightest familiar trigger can send the whole system into a downward spiral.

We are a bright lot. We are so rational and yet we are often so wrong. Our razor-sharp ability to logic can keep us stuck in realities so vivid and limiting that we don't even realize they are of our own making. I often think that I will have to literally pry my own mind open in order to cease its rigid preoccupation and allow relief. In truth, just interrupting the old negative thought patterns will bring back the meaning we seek in moments like these. Aligning our minds with the most compassionate words and thoughts we can muster can bring connection and a sense of peace. For some, it means giving up almost an entire way of life, but only this will allow glints of joy to shine through.

I remember once suggesting to a client that his life could be fun. It was such an insult to his intelligence that he walked out of my office never to return. I was fired. It struck me just as funny then as it does now. I had assaulted him in a way I would have never thought was an assault. It was a mere suggestion, but it was mind-bending to him. You would have thought I was trying to convert him to a bizarre new religion.

To live a life of meaning, at some point, we have to decide to arm-wrestle with our minds. It can take years of analysis and psychotherapy. On the other hand, we could also surrender our minds to a higher power. Sheer willpower is an option, surely. Or we can focus on making conscious choices in every moment.

Our mind is malleable. Often the brain needs better stimulation than what we've been giving it. As I've learned through my son's epilepsy, when you allow the brain to continue to malfunction, it trains itself to repeat the problem over and over. Without the medication or diet that stops the misfiring, the brain will just continue to malfunction. We have to stop the habit and divert the brain's impulse so we can cause a positive synapse to occur. For those of us who don't have a brain ailment other than our own thinking, it requires retraining. For some of us it's a walk in the park, and for some of us it's a triathlon, but for all of us, our very malleable brains *will* do what we program them to do.

The mind is its own place, and in itself,
Can make Heaven of Hell, a Hell of Heaven.
—John Milton

~ ~ ~

Dearest Universal Intelligence, help me tap into the greater flow of collective goodness to train my own mind. Allow me the strength to overcome the habits of my mind that do not yield life-affirming thoughts. Help me embrace the power to transcend my own mind. Bless me with the sight that allows me to see good in all I do and experience. May I hold myself and others in my mind's eye as whole, good, and complete.

~ ~ ~

ELEVEN

Re-Mind Me

I've battled depression for most of my adult life. I don't discuss it much, but when I do, as now, it's to encourage someone suffering from depression. The response is usually one of surprise, like "You seem so energetic and positive!"

"That's my nature," I respond. "And I have to fight for it every day."

My most debilitating bout with depression was in my twenties, but I've been managing the aftershocks of depression for twenty years. Intrusive thoughts, mental dullness, self-directed anger, and days of sadness still pass through like unwanted freight trains at a crossing when you have somewhere to go.

The big D doesn't rule my life anymore, but it sits

right under the surface like vermin watching the action aboveground from a sewer drain. It lurks at street level in line with the lowest vantage point as I walk above, seeing the sun and breathing cleaner air, being very careful not to fall into a hole and meet up with it. Oddly, it has brought tremendous meaning to my life as I have learned how to be very conscious of my thoughts and choose them differently, if need be. If I've learned one thing, it is that just because I think something doesn't mean I have to believe it. I saw a bumper sticker the other day that captured my motto: *Don't believe everything you think.*

The Buddha said that all suffering is due to attachment. It is the mind that causes attachment. It is the mind that concocts an ironclad argument about how we are right or how we've been wronged or about how the world operates, and it is such that creates the cell that isolates us. We have made up our mind or it has been made up for us. The good news is that we can change it. We can be re-minded. To heal our perception is to give birth to freedom and meaning.

We are all faced with choices, whether we battle depression or not. Do we allow ourselves to be fear-minded, anxiety driven, scarcity-minded? Do we allow anger, hurt, and resentment to rule our minds? Do we dig ourselves deep into a trench and fight all the time causing ourselves great stress, even for a "good" cause like a pay-check? Do we linger in the glory of our discontent? Any of these mental states involve a choice on our part. It's not simple to make the choice, unfortunately—there may be work needed in therapy to unravel the root beliefs—but it is absolutely possible to free ourselves from fearful and angry thoughts to embrace thoughts that nurture love and connection. What's interesting is that some of the smartest people with the most developed minds suffer the most at the hand of their own high analytical ability when it comes to having happiness and meaning in their life. These often black-and-white thinkers, who see very little that is gray or colorful, are highly and quickly deci-sive but can also easily miss joy in the way they process. Quick to decide what is good and what is bad, little room is left for mystery and discovery and some of the other elements that slow us down long enough to feel meaning.

Imagine an executive gets the sense something fishy is going on at work; information is being kept from her. People stop when she enters a room. She notices a few funny looks and closed-door meetings that would not normally happen. Agitated and suspicious, she snaps at her husband and kids, wonders aloud what's going on? She's afraid she is going to be fired.

At the beginning of the third week of this strangeness,

she walks into work and finds the place strangely quiet. She peeks into a couple of empty offices. This is it, she thinks, they're all meeting somewhere without me, about my future. Determined to find out what is happening, she opens a conference room door; there's an explosion of laughter. Her momentary shock clears as she deciphers the chorus of Happy Birthday wishes. It's her fiftieth birthday and her coworkers and staff have thrown her a surprise birthday party breakfast. Even her kids are there.

Clearly the star of our story had misinterpreted the meaning of the secrecy filtering through her office setting. How many times do we misinterpret the things we see and hear in our own lives? How often do we stack the cards against ourselves through our interpretation of events, robbing ourselves of what can be meaningful in the name of fear?

Back in my days as a performer, I had put myself in an environment that fed on my propensity for negative thinking and fear. I remember an audition for *Little Shop of Horrors*, one of my favorite shows. It was probably for some summer stock because I was impossibly young at the time to play the lead, Audrey, in a top-notch production. I waited on line with the rest of the hopefuls in a rehearsal hall on West Fifteenth Street in Manhattan.

As my turn drew near, I shed my red cowboy boots for a pair of patent-leather five-inch pumps, and primped my black, flounced skirt. Audrey had what you might call hooker taste in clothes. I had just understudied the lead in the Philadelphia company of the Broadway production, so I felt I was a shoo-in to get this role in this lesser venue. My voice was warmed up and I knew the music cold. My turn came and I went in.

The room was spacious and the floors were new. The honey-colored wood reflected light from the ceiling-high windows along one side of the studio. I made my way to the far end of the room and took my mark. The two men at a table gave me the signal to start singing.

I give it my all and I'm sounding pretty damn good (I thought), and then I realize my two-person audience is not paying attention. One guy put his finger down his throat as if gagging himself and then across his neck as if slashing it. Finally, he pulled a newspaper in front of him and held it up so I was shielded from whatever else he needed to discuss with his colleague. Neither of them stopped me or looked at me, and as I kept singing I felt a huge lump building in my throat. This went on for an eternity. At last the song was over. The two said their perfunctory "Thank you" and sent me on my way.

I maneuvered the crowded hall of hopefuls and endured

their inquiries as to how it went. Most people don't care how it went; they want to pick up whatever they can use to get the part. I didn't say a word: I shed my pumps, pulled on my cowboy boots, and went home to cry.

I was ashamed that I was reduced to a pillow wetting, crying heap, but I was. Hoping to talk my way out of the feelings, I called my mother, who was empathetic. After enduring my outpouring of hurt, she said: "For all you know, you reminded him of his ex-wife."

That was a strange thing to say but even stranger was—it made me feel better! I snapped out of my funk, realizing that I had the choice to not interpret this rejection as an indictment of my talent, my future, or my personal worth. I could choose to forget the gagging gesture and go on to audition, which is exactly what I did for several more years. Re-minding myself gave me staying power, although I did leave the business eventually.

When things do not go our way, it is easy to believe the mind's condemnations. By doing so, we put ourselves into a far deeper hell than the true event could possibly cause. To avoid that hell is to choose to be re-minded. It is a chance to question our disappointment or pain or resentment, and to stop assuming what we think is the truth.

We could all stand to be reminded of our true essence.

We are love, in essence. We are goodness at our core. When we can download that truth into our minds, we have what *A Course in Miracles* calls the Christ Mind. For non-Christians, that moniker can be hard to swallow, but as I see it, it means that we think and see as Jesus did. He saw love and goodness in everyone. He was not afraid to connect with that essence in all beings, no matter how they looked, smelled, or instilled fear in others. The Christ Mind is a loving, forgiving mind-set. Forget the name. We could all use a little re-minding; we need to be re-minded of who we really are.

To help me stop believing what I thought, I took a hiatus in my twenties from journal writing for an entire year. Diaries and journals, such a traditional ode to woe and a place to store and visit our innermost thoughts, are often therapeutic. But I had realized that mine were volumes of whining that were reinforcing my unhealthy thoughts. My best therapy was refusing to write in mine until I could write something positive. What a revelation!

That is the power of our mind. So magnificent, so intelligent, so naturally a miracle in the umpteen processes and functions it is able to carry out, and yet we are subjective creatures and we interpret the meaning of events in our lives from a very slanted view. Those interpretations often disconnect us from experiencing true meaning. The power of our own minds to distort meaning or create meaning is unending, and in fact will never completely go away, as that's the way our brains work. To use it for good instead of ill, especially toward ourselves, opens up the possibility to embrace more meaning and significance in our lives. To end the focus on what is wrong or not working is to open the mind to all those things that we've established that can create connection and, therefore, meaning. To be free to connect with beauty, each other, possibility, and ease is the key to peace. From peace all can be and grow as it should—as it's meant to.

I started my mental shift—something that has become more common knowledge in recent years—by drawing from one of the deepest wells the mind can dip from, gratitude. To draw on gratitude is to feel grace filling one's heart and overflowing into the bloodstream until it becomes a mood and then an action and, finally, a way of life. It can turn the pain of thinking into the joy of being.

For me, in the throes of a deep depression, in the darkness of my apartment, after lighting a candle in the small, hall-like bathroom and praying for the crying to stop, there was a moment, like a hiccup, that interrupted my train of thought and caused me to move off the cold bathroom floor and into the studio. I lay down on the hardwood floor. I had a keen sense that it was time to find something to be thankful for. In retrospect, I can see there was so much that could have been listed, but in my state of mind, I was devoid of a thankful thought. I struggled to hear a grateful thought, and finally one came.

I am grateful that I have ten fingers and toes.

That was it. That's all I could think of. But I focused on that. That led to the next thought.

I am grateful for my body that works well.

And then another.

I am grateful that I am healthy.

And another.

I am grateful that I have food to eat.

It was starting to flow, but if it felt too pushed or forced, I'd start to feel like a phony and get angry. That would wreck the whole thing and I'd have to start all over again by going back to something I could truly be grateful for. Despite the setbacks, it was there, on the inlaid floor, that I started to change my mind. As gratitude started to melt the faulty thinking that had kept me stuck, the darkness gave way to glimmers and moments of lightness. In those moments, the bad stuff stopped feeling permanent and possibilities found their way into the open spots in my mind to deposit hope and faith in myself. Each peek into the light would multiply upon itself until it was more and more reinforced by new thinking, eventually resulting in my being re-minded. It took much attention, focus, and patience. I persisted until I could finally stop watching each thought and could begin to trust my own thoughts to be supportive versus destructive. It took months.

Having so much attention on my thoughts was like living in an altered universe where time stood still and the volume was too loud in my own head. Walking through the world felt like a dream, because I was so focused on what was going on in my head and in my mind that I was barely awake in the daily transaction of my life. It was an alternative reality to be so heavily aware of my thoughts.

Not everyone has to start as far down the thought food chain as I did to be re-minded. Anything or anyone we need to champion requires us to find more evidence on the side of the good versus the destructive. I had to use the same level of mental attention to champion other decisions in my life. There was a time when my sick, frightened ego mind was trying to keep me unhappy and lonely by attempting to sabotage my engagement to Mark.

He has no money.

He has no prospects for the future.

He is not movie-star gorgeous! (Like I *was*, please!)

I fought back hard against these thoughts with:

I have never known unconditional love like he gives me.
He makes my heart sing.
He believes in me one hundred percent.
He's gorgeous in so many ways.

Whether we need to champion an unpopular decision, our child, our marriage, or ourselves, winning the battle of the mind is first and then the action follows. But we need to find the wisdom to champion the side that moves us forward and fuels us, not the side that keep us fearful, limited, and stuck. How much time is wasted in choosing to remain paralyzed? Or negative? Or in continuing to suffer and be disconnected from meaning? Too much. How many times have we wasted precious hours to worry and anxiety and being sure that a situation is as we perceive it, only to find out we were wrong? Think of all the time that we could have been anxiety-free and contributing in a meaningful way.

The power of our thoughts is evident on the opposite side of the equation too. It certainly isn't only negative thoughts that can throw us off center. I've noticed in yoga class that if my mind latches on to my performance, especially if I think I'm doing well, I'll fall off balance or lose the thread of my breath. There I'll be, feeling weightless and otherworldly in a Warrior Three, balanced on one leg, leaning over with my gaze to the floor, arms outstretched in front of me, and I'll think: "You are doing really well. This is good." Next thing I know, I am bouncing one hand off the floor a few times as I try to regain center. I re-mind myself by returning to whatever I dedicated my practice to at the beginning of class—often the health and well-being of my children—or I dedicate my strength to someone who needs it.

Yoga is a physical, mental, and spiritual practice that brings connection and alignment to self. It can be an incredibly meaningful exercise when the yoga mat is a place to meet oneself. What we think on the mat is what we think off the mat. One of my teachers said recently: "The moment when you want to release a pose early [before the instruction], the yoga really begins." If we're judgmental on the mat, we're probably judgmental in day-to-day life. If we want to quit on the mat when the going gets rough, we likely do the same in life. If our self-criticism is harsh as we learn the poses, it's likely we'll suffer the same fate in other parts of life. To be re-minded in a practice like yoga is to learn to surrender to what is in the moment without judging it. If our mind gets stuck during the practice, attached to some thought, good or bad, the practice falls out of flow. The same thing is true for our everyday life. The flow is smooth when the mind remains open and present to all that is happening and all you are doing, and falls away from meaningful flow when you judge what is happening, good or bad.

Breathing and the control of our breath is also a big part of a yogi's practice. My teacher's comparisons continue. She said: "How we breathe on the mat reflects our state of mind." What that means is if we are panting and out of control in our breathing, we are likely to be the same in our adrenaline-filled day. When we can use our breath fully and in a way where we are truly nourished by the oxygen we take in, we are able to allow ourselves to melt into being present. That calm allows for clearer thinking and better decision making. It may even allow us to dissipate many problems before they even begin. We have a longer wick before something may ignite our temper or a strong emotion. We can avoid dramas when we have that kind of psychic and emotional space in our life. It is that cushion of emotional space between us and our world that allows us to recognize meaning in everyday things. We stop reacting and have time to choose our responses. We are re-minded.

With the mind calm and the breath steady, we are opened like a geode. We can be ready to shine what is spectacular about us and receive what can help us show our brilliance.

TWELVE

Meditate, Meditate, Meditate

I began teaching myself to meditate in the late eighties, before the "dark curtain" fell on the first act of my life. I was drawn to meditate partly because I was young and impressionable—it was the good New Age thing to do. I also thought it made me cool and artsy. But by not having a good instructor or a meditation tape (or even some good New Age music!), I found myself having some crazy meditative journeys before I came to understand the essential skill of stillness.

One particular day I sat on the fire escape of the cast house of a theater where I was working in the Poconos. It was a hot summer's day, hosting only a hint of a breeze. The sun felt nourishing and the perch where I sat made me feel like I was suspended over the ground with nothing impeding me from flight. I closed my eyes and breathed in the delicious air allowing it to make me slightly light-headed. My attention fell on a friend who had left the company a few days prior and who I was already missing. Before I could really be conscious of any decisions I was making about what this meditation might be like, with my eyes closed, I began feeling like I was traveling through the air to visit my friend in his New York City apartment, seventy-five miles away. In my mind's eye, I could see the farms, cornfields, the highway, the suburbs, and the city as I traveled the route to his apartment. It was exhilarating. I began to breathe more deeply and freely, a sense of well-being spread over me like hot wax coating a car at the car wash. While I was at it, I decided I'd "check in" on my apartment and some other friends while I was in the neighborhood. By the time I came back to my spot on the fire escape, fifteen or twenty minutes had gone by. I had an odd sense of accomplishment—like I had done something. I didn't know if that was what meditation was supposed to be like, but I liked it and felt good for the rest of the day.

Now I know to call what I did visualization—a meditative journey that includes seeing something in your mind's eye or following a suggestion from yourself, someone else, or a tape to reach a meditative state through a visual experience. That's just one way, but there are many.

Our culture is increasingly aware of meditation, but actually knowing how to practice it is still an unsolved riddle to most. Since most have not experienced the benefits, it is hard to motivate people to try and, even more important, to stick with a practice over time. Yes, we intellectually know it has a calming effect, can improve our health, and promote clearer thinking, but those haven't been compelling enough reasons for most people to actually do it. In our exploration of meaning, meditation offers a powerful way to quiet the mind so connection and oneness can prevail. It can help bring the power of the peaceful mind to the forefront instead of continuing to be beholden to the critical mind that wants to keep us separate and miserable.

Beginning meditators fall asleep. They get up to pee a hundred times. They think of something that needs to get done and fool themselves into thinking that if they just get up right then and do it, get it out of the way, another to-do won't crop up next time they try to sit to meditate. I've heard people say, "I can't sit still. I'm one of those people who always needs to be doing *something*." Or, "Meditation, it's not my thing." It's not for everyone, clearly, but I think most who dismiss it, generally speaking, aren't fully aware of what is really keeping them from it.

What awaits us in the silence is ourselves. Not a lot of

people want to meet themselves in this space of nothing-
ness. I can't say what they fear specifically, but I can make
some educated guesses. We fear something—our own
shadow, so to speak, or the vastness of nothing, the fear
of stopping and feeling everything that we haven't had
time to feel or discovering that we are more or less than
what we thought we were.

I remember a client who was struggling to come to
some understanding of his life and what he wanted to do
with it. He had trouble doing nothing and I felt that was
part of what was blocking him from getting clear about
what he wanted to do with his life. During one phone
session, I remember hearing him smoking. I could hear
him taking drags off the cigarette in the pauses of our
conversation. When I asked him to not smoke on our
calls, he replaced smoking with drinking, made obvious
by clinking ice cubes. I asked him to stop numbing himself during our sessions. He agreed, and yet the next time
we spoke, I could hear the TV in the background. When
I pointed this out, he explained that he always leaves it on
because he hates being truly alone. At one point, he asked
me to help him learn how to meditate. Getting him to sit
still was like asking a flea not to jump onto the nearest
fuzzy surface. To his credit, he tried.

What finally worked for him was walking his dog. He

did that anyway, but he found a new meditative awareness by noticing nature and taking in more of the natural wonder around him. Before, he obsessed over what kind of cars his neighbors had and what was on his to-do list that day. With practice, he eventually learned to bring his new calm indoors to sit and be with himself in total silence.

What are we avoiding by not being with ourselves? Acceptance of what is, whether we like what's happening or not? Meeting all the parts of ourselves we pretend are not there or the parts we'd like to think are not wounded? Truth can be a scary destination. But getting to the truth and living through the discovery allows us to set the stage for meaning. When our energy is not consumed by efforts to uphold a fabrication about who we are or what we'd like things to be like, we are finally free to connect to ourselves and others. We can then move through life and problems with more grace and, perhaps, patience.

When I first met myself after trying to avoid doing so for years, I cried. No, I sobbed. I felt incredibly sorry for who I met. That person was in so much pain. I thought I was going to meet a lot of anger if I sat in silence with myself. I was expecting to be as angry with myself as I was in my walking-waking hours of the day. That's why I had avoided meditating. But there was no anger—only empathy for this person who had robbed herself of being happy because of a set of rules she operated by. In the stillness, I saw myself through a more forgiving heart. It felt like nothing short of a miracle.

It took me about another five years to experience the deeper benefits of quieting my mind through meditation. Many times my attempts led me only to nap. But I never gave up completely, and in retrospect I can say that even the times I fell asleep were part of the process of learning how to meditate effectively. More recently, having three kids has made meditating tougher, but the scarcity of time has only improved my ability to turn off my mind's chatter with the flick of an eyelash. Getting to nothing is easy now. The hard part is remembering to go there, but when I do, it's such a relief.

When I close my eyes, I feel the gentle pressure of my eyes behind my eyelids, which I also feel as a gentle pressure at the bridge of my nose—right between the eyes. To teach people what I mean, I ask them to put their forefinger pointing directly at that spot on the bridge of their nose where it meets their forehead. That pressure is like a light switch in speed and it makes your mind go blank for a moment. That sensation is what I equate with a successful meditation. The trick is to keep that blankness going for as long as you can. I may still hear birds chirping or air conditioners humming, but as long as my mind does not switch back on and begin processing thoughts it stays in meditation. For me, it can happen now by just closing my eyes with the intent to feel that "blank." Getting up from a time in "blank" snaps me back into feeling fully alive. I can be overtired or sad or overcaffeinated and come out of the "blank" energized and even-keeled. It's taken many, many years to get here, but I remember feeling helped by every attempt at meditating from the early naps that overtook me to using tapes to using mantras—all of it. Everyone has to find his own "way."

During the question-and-answer period at a Marianne Williamson lecture that I attended when I was in my twenties, almost every response from Marianne to any question or concern from the audience was "Meditate, meditate, meditate!" delivered in an Asian Indian accent. It was funny and it was a great answer. If we sit quietly with a problem long enough, we will eventually connect with the wisdom that allows us to uncover the answer or solution. We will find our own meaning out of troublesome events or problems in the silence. Unfortunately, the answer cannot be rushed, and that's a bummer if you have a pressing deadline.

Osho, a Hindu philosopher and mystic who died in 1990, tells a story about the Buddha. Three different people come to him with questions about God. (It's important to note that the Buddhist tradition exists in the absence of a creator God.) The first man asks, "Does God exist?" to which the Buddha answers yes, because he knows that the man is an atheist and he wants him to be challenged in his belief. The second man asks, "Is there a God?" and the Buddha answers, "No, not at all," knowing that the man is looking for confirmation of his own belief; the Buddha would not dictate any one belief. The third man humbly asks the Buddha, "Would you say something about God?" to which the Buddha replies by closing his eyes and sitting in silence. The man joins the Buddha and after half an hour gets up and touches the Buddha's feet and says: "Thank you for your answer."

The Buddha's elder cousin watches all these exchanges and is bubbling over with confusion—how can the Buddha give contradictory answers to the questions? When he asks, the Buddha explains that he has answered according to what each person brought to the question. The last man, the Buddha says, was the wisest, for he knew to be still with the question. "And you are puzzled about what answer he thanked me for? He received the answer that silence is divine, and to be silent is to be godly; there is no other god than silence. He went away tremendously fulfilled, contented. He has found the answer. I have not given him the answer; he found the answer. I simply allowed him to have a taste of my presence."[1]

That last statement could sound egotistical on the Buddha's part, but I interpret what he means by presence as not his actual being but his ability to be fully "there" in the moment that influenced the visiting man to be able to do the same, which in turn led to his answer.

Quieting the mind reveals meaning because it fosters connection to self, emotion, motivation, and it helps us join instead of separate or push away feelings. Meditation lights up the prefrontal cortex where feelings of compassion, intuition, and empathy occur. It turns on our "sympathetic" brain. The brain wave pattern created during meditation can bring on feelings of well-being and overall wellness. The brain waves created when we think, plan, scheme, and worry do not.

Richard Davidson, a prominent neuroscience professor at the University of Wisconsin–Madison, measured the brain waves of sixteen Tibetan Buddhist monks. The outcome was so unbelievable he checked to be certain his MRI and other brain-marking machinery were not malfunctioning by bringing in a group of students

[1]Osho, *The Spiritual Path: Buddha, Zen, Tao, Tantra* (Lewes, England: Ivy Press, 2005).

as a control group. The gamma waves emanated by the monks were thirty times as strong as those produced by the control group. The study showed that the more experienced the monk, the greater his brain's plasticity and its ability to sustain positive qualities such as compassion, peace, and contentment reached during meditation during nonmeditative times. True, these monks were logging ten thousand to fifty thousand hours of meditation practice over their lifetimes,[2] so we have to ask, is it possible for us "regular" meditators to touch that same quiet, the same emptiness, and bring it into daily life? Yes, I believe so. And yet I wonder how to be truthful without saying what it feels like. What are we to look for? I can say what I believe to be success, and that is when the thoughts stop: when there is nothing left to think; when nothing registers in my mind or anywhere in my body as something to think about or examine; when there is a blank—not as when your mind draws a blank and you instantly panic and start searching for what you meant to say—but I mean blank, nothing—and a sensation that the absence of feeling and thinking is acceptable. That, in fact, it is desired.

[2]Study details reported in Sharon Begley, "The Lotus and the Synapse," Newsweek.com.

When we talk about meaning, we can be in a thinking mode about it. Choosing what something means, accepting what something means, or experiencing the connection that fills us with a sense of purpose and meaning—and yet meditation takes us beyond the thinking or feeling to a connection to nothing (and everything) that allows the ultimate ability to avail ourselves to everything and anything.

It is hard to describe the place where thinking and nature meet—where we are not in control, but rather just a part of the scene or experience and therefore experiencing an "emptiness," as the Buddhists call it. Seeing the emptiness as a positive is the modern challenge. The emptiness is the place where anything is possible and where our relationship to ourselves, our life, others, and our world can start again. It's as if the place that we can reach through meditation is one where we can let go of the past and stop anticipating the future and be open and without judgment. This is what allows us to be more accurate and a clearer perceiver of meaning.

The access to pure meaning, meaning through "being" (versus contrived meaning, meaning through "thinking"), comes from this emptiness. The mind needs to understand its place as part of our survival mechanism. It is not the be-all and end-all center of our existence and truth.

THIRTEEN

Shut Your Mouth

I speak for a living. And yet for me, the greatest meaning has come from learning to shut my mouth.

To quiet the mind, we need to shut our mouths. Once we do, what we are thinking backs up into the brain. But this is not a bad thing, as when a sink's drain gets backed up, stopping the flow of water. When the mind holds back a thought that should not come out, the thought will often dissipate until it loses its importance and no longer needs to be spoken. If the thoughts are unkind, with a watchful awareness, they can melt into kindness. When that happens, connection—ironically, the reason most of us open our mouth in the first place—can actually occur. We think talking connects. It does to a point, but a greater connection can come from the silence. In that connection, we find meaning: we understand, we get clear, we feel love, we tap compassion, we get answers, and we feel *well*.

One of the retreats required for my seminary training took place at a monastery overlooking the Hudson River, New York City just out of sight. In the midst of our weekend retreat, we were assigned an afternoon of silence. We were not to talk to anyone—not even during meals. As the instructions were being shared, I could barely sit still, overcome with excitement by the thought of being freed of the burden of talking. It was as if someone had given me a huge present. I was so happy. I could feel my body tingling and then relaxing as I accepted having permission to do and say nothing.

The students were dismissed to begin their silent time and I found myself drawn to the chapel. I don't often seek out a sanctuary unless I am in a foreign country where the deep, rich history seems to beckon me to the doors. So I was curious as I watched myself drawn to sit in a pew in a Christian chapel. I let the silence fill me. The next thing I knew, I was kneeling in front of a modern, Picassoesque wood carving of Mary, Jesus' mother. Then I began to cry.

I'd never felt a connection to the image of Mary before, but to be truly free to be quiet, I had to hand over my children to Mary. It felt as weird to me as it sounds. I was having an otherworldly experience as I charged her with babysitting my three kids, who were not even on site with me, so I could truly let go, take this break, and enter the silent world. I could feel a spiritual and mental exchange in which Mary took my kids. She "had" them. The vigilance left my body and I was free to "be." With the transfer of their care, my silent retreat had truly begun.

The monastery sported a rolling backyard that ended at a cliff overlooking the Hudson. It was a New York version of the scene in *The Sound of Music* where Sister Maria dances through the hills. I didn't do it but I pictured myself dancing across the grass. Instead, I walked, arms outstretched, breathing in the air to my fullest capacity. High on oxygen, life, and silence, I made my way over to the labyrinth set up on the property.

New to labyrinths at the time, all I knew was that you were to choose a question, quandary, or intention to keep in your mind and heart as you walked the path. On the way in, you keep your focus in mind and on the way out, an answer, a revelation, or a next step might occur to you. Ancient and modern mystics use labyrinths to achieve a contemplative state. I don't remember what question I brought into the labyrinth, but I do remember that as I exited I was laughing inside, because an idea for a comedy bit about seminary was coming to me that I could deliver later at our open-mike talent night. I scurried to my dormitory to write down my thoughts.

My room had cinder-block walls. It sported cheap carpeting, a twin bed, a desk, small armchair, and oh, let's not forget Jesus on the cross. He looked cold and miserable on that bare wall. The room was hardly warm and cozy, but it was functional enough that I felt safe in its simplicity. I entertained myself there by writing my stand-up routine for that night. It's important to note that although I had been a performer, and I use humor when I teach and give keynotes, I do *not* do stand-up. Anything scripted is a recipe for failure for me. Funny disappears from my being, just as people lose the color in their face when they see a ghost. Scripted Laura equals not-funny Laura. So, although I was cracking myself up and enjoying a laughfest in my mind, I had enough logic left to question the sanity of what I was attempting to prepare for that evening's show. But the joy was almost more than I could bear.

The dinner hour was the final sixty minutes of our silent interlude. It was powerfully obvious how we rely on talking over a meal. It's a ritual in itself. Without it, it was odd, but transforming. I ate slower. I tasted every morsel. I ate less and got full quicker and my heart seemed to swell to the size of my plate. Being with other people without words meant looking at each other deeply. Not hearing them, I was left to feel them. To feel them was to feel my heart expand, to have kindness take over and to radiate and receive warmth. My mind was quiet and any judgment was gone. This experience was not new to me, but it was brought home again that this is where the connection that we crave lies.

The people I went to seminary with, all of them in that dining hall, felt so dear to me. There was George, his cherubic face like a medieval monk's. His gentleness envelops anyone who meets his eye. There was Madeline, a petite powerhouse in her sixties, whom you could confuse for a crazy eccentric but who is really a wise woman whose words wrap ribbons around anyone who listens. And Mary Oriolla, the embodiment of a Yoruba priestess, with long neck and arms, and hands so graceful that every move she makes is a dance. I had little in common with a lot of them and everything in common with all of them. We shared a human experience and silence helped me meet them there. When we are done talking, being awaits and meaning grows.

When I could talk again, I was emceeing the talent night and scored a hit with my comedy bits. A first! One I think made possible only by an abundance of closed lips.

Closed lips, open heart; open heart, quiet mind.

There is a lovely quotation from Sai Baba of Shirdi, an Indian man regarded by both Hindu and Muslim followers as a saint: "Before you speak, ask yourself, is it kind, is it necessary, is it true, does it improve on the silence?" Sai Baba's advice has been a great litmus test for me. Will my words improve on the silence? That's tough for a speaker who thinks she has something to say and for someone who spent the first half of her life as a gossip.

When I was in my twenties and first discovered Marianne Williamson's lectures in New York City, I remember her suggesting one night that gossiping was a no-no. She had been known for years as a spiritual teacher and leader. Hearing her say that was like getting an arrow between my eyes.

"What the heck would I talk about?" I thought. "How would I have conversations if I didn't talk about other people?" I was dumbfounded for months, then suddenly there was a new consciousness about the shallowness of my former existence. I was acutely aware of how judgmental I had been, often masquerading as the fashion police. I would walk down the street in horror and disgust, as I had to endure the fashion choices and unfortunate and uneven distribution of beauty in the world. My mind was very busy judging.

Why would she wear that? That's disgusting.
Oh, please! Didn't anyone tell him the sixties are over?
What a pig. That dress is way too tight.
He's a jerk, just look at him. Oh, God!

I thought I knew a lot—a lot more than other people, anyway. I was right and painfully, acutely perceptive and smart. What the hell was this newfound guilt around sharing my views and judgments? Who would save the world from its awful, fashion-challenged, clueless self?

I did begin to see how destructive my thinking and my mind could be, how gossip was another form of separation, devoid of true meaning. I slowly made different choices. About four years after this, when I was in training to become a professional coach and the next level of challenge was presented to me, the definition of gossip changed. It was no longer just speaking about other people in a negative context. My mentor suggested that a new line to tow was to uphold that speaking about anyone who was not present was also considered gossip, regardless of positive or negative content.

"Damn!" I thought. "Now I can't even share other people's good news?" It was like starting all over again. It wasn't that any of this made me a terrible person, but it did bring my motivation into question. When I told someone else's good news, wasn't I stealing his or her thunder? Shouldn't they get to tell people themselves? Who was the winner if I used my mouth irresponsibly? My ego. That was the honest answer. So it was time to change. Again.

I can still talk an evil blue streak when provoked, but my mind quieted greatly once I learned to keep my mouth shut. As it turns out, that old saying "If you don't have anything nice to say, don't say it" is not so trite after all. For me there's another one that keeps me humble: "Small minds discuss people, average minds discuss events, and great minds discuss ideas." It's often a stretch, but it guides me out of trouble.

It's odd how so many of us struggle with what to say, especially when we are trying to say something meaningful. Sharing our love, our sorrow for a mourner, our pride in a child, or even an accolade for a coworker. It's interesting how the words are right there when we are quick to anger and yet elusive when we feel effusive. In anger we connect with the feeling and don't have time to measure our words. In love, many of us flee mentally. We hatch the emotion we want to communicate at a higher level of consciousness and then we seem to slide down the scale and go a bit unconscious, getting nervous and self-conscious.

In truth, it may be that words fall short to describe

our enlightened moments. There are no words for a state that is word-free. Words may not always be the bridge to understanding ourselves or someone else. Being quiet of mind and connecting silently will intensify the connection and raise the volume on loving thoughts. There will be no gap between you. The meaning will be there.

Now, to ponder whether any of this relates to my daughter's latest request of me: "Can you please shut your mouth when you chew your gum?"

FOURTEEN

Judge Me Not

I had been waiting for my delayed flight to board after a long four-day stretch of work. I had given a weekend workshop with an almost nonexistent voice because of a cold, and just in the nick of time had gotten my voice back to deliver a Tuesday-morning keynote five hundred miles away. Now I was on my way home. I was so happy to learn I had been upgraded to first class. As I waited among the throngs of stranded travelers, my phone rang. It was one of my dearest friends, whom I had not been able to reach for almost two weeks. The chase to find her started when I had heard that wildfires in San Diego were threatening to ravage hundreds of homes in her area. It was an awkward time to take the call, but I needed to talk to her.

I was pretty stressed under the circumstances, and being on the phone while I juggled high heels, my luggage, and my boarding pass and dealt with the gate agent was making me sweat. I had broken my own rules to be talking on the phone while trying to deal with another human being, but my friend had been through a terrible ordeal.

I was so happy to finally settle into my big seat and focus on my friend.

"We left the house with flames bouncing off our roof," she said. "Luckily, the computers were right by the front door, so we grabbed them, our shoes, and the dog and piled into the car. I had left my cell phone next to my bed and just got it back, that's why you didn't hear from me."

Because of an inaccurate report from the police department that her house had been destroyed, she lived for days with the idea that she had lost her home. As it turned out, her house had not been destroyed, but her in-laws lost their house, and she lost her second home. She was now living in a motel.

As I sat with my mouth open in disbelief at what I was hearing, a man suddenly stuck his ticket in my face. He was sweaty and exasperated, and he kept shoving his ticket at me. I did not think I was in the wrong seat, but I asked my friend to hold on so I could see what he wanted.

"You need to move so my daughter and I can sit together," he said.

He was clearly stressed, and if I had had my wits about me, I would have asked him to wait a minute so I could hang up, but I did not want to leave my friend. I looked at his ticket stub and in my own stress blurted with a sigh that I hated the bulkhead seat—where he had wanted me to move. He didn't even give me a chance to explore the options we had before he called me an asshole. He had said it softly, but I am not one to tolerate passive-aggressive behavior, so in a very loud voice I repeated what he said:

"Now he's calling me an asshole!" I boomed.

As I said good-bye to my friend, the man found another solution for himself and his daughter. My distaste for the bulkhead didn't mean I was not going to move if necessary. I too am a parent who has been in the same situation. I have a long flying history of moving and sitting in the worst seats to get parents together with their kids.

I got up and walked over to the man, now settled just fine with his daughter, who must have been around seven or eight. I was calm.

"Listen, I don't appreciate the name-calling and you judging me, assuming that you know who I am as a person because of what just happened."

"Oh, I know who you are," he said with disdain and disgust. "You are the kind of despicable person who would separate a father from his child and make her fly alone."

I knew this was going to be futile, but I was hoping I could give the man some perspective of where my head was at when he shoved his ticket in my face. (And he never asked me to move—he *told* me to.)

"I was on the phone with a friend who lost homes in the San Diego fires."

He shut up. For a moment.

I went back to my seat, but I could feel this man's eyes on me. The next installment of his rage came when a passenger stood in the aisle, confused as to why someone was in his seat. The angry man had taken the empty seat to be with his daughter, and loudly explained to the new passenger:

"That *lovely* lady over there would not accommodate us, so we had to move your seat," he said with the greatest of sarcasm.

By now, I was shaking because I had nowhere to process what I was feeling. I called my husband. I was still feeling the sting of his condemnation, but my husband pointed out that this man had judged me, tried his best to publicly humiliate me, and was being unforgiving. What was he modeling for his daughter? Perhaps he wanted to teach her that you get what you want by name-calling, bullying, humiliating, and making a fuss as loudly as you can.

The man continued to send barbs my way any chance he got until well into the flight. The other passengers averted their eyes and said nothing from the very beginning. His other daughter and his wife, who were sitting in coach, kept coming up to visit until the flight attendant asked them to please stop because they were getting in the way of her doing her job. (No comment.)

I felt the normal, human pull to want to annihilate this person. The moment never came for another verbal tangle, and perhaps it was for the best because I was not yet out of judgment mode myself. Later, I happened upon the following words that spoke to my situation:

> A superior being does not render evil for evil. . . . A noble soul is always compassionate, even toward those who enjoy injuring others or who are actually committing cruel deeds—for who is without fault?
>
> —from the *Ramayana*

In moments of "right-mindedness" on that flight, I knew the guy was stressed and concerned for his child. I understood where he was coming from. And as much as I told myself not to take it personally, the righteousness he showed made me angry.

The "Righteous," those who profess a higher morality, have a long history of causing pain with their judgment. Those who condemn often derive great meaning for their lives by being moral yardsticks. When we judge, we condemn and find someone guilty of doing wrong. A life of condemning others can fill us with power and superiority. When we succumb to this temporary fluffing-up of our ego—the peacock strut or the lion's roar—we mistake a feeling of superiority with rightness. Somehow, to know more or be better than somebody else seems right, when really it is more cause for separation from others, and therefore, a great source of meaning in our lives.

Carl Jung said: "Condemnation does not liberate, it oppresses." When we point to another person's frailties with the aim of "putting them in their place," we annihilate what could potentially be a good and whole relationship based on trust. As noted in 1 Corinthians 4:14 (*The Living Bible*), "Correction is helpful when it is motivated by love rather than condemnation." Sometimes we even fool ourselves into thinking that we are offering our judgment in order to "help" the other person—we need to look long and hard at our motivations. Is this coming from love?

When we feel justified, in the right, and above judgment ourselves, we think we have reached some pinnacle of perfection. But if we notice what judgment does, we see that it moves people like the weights on a shuffleboard—some on one end and the rest on the other. It separates us, pushing one side to the supposedly superior "in the club" position and the other to one that is left out, lacking. Meaning does not come from separation, and when we think it does, it's because the ego has told us so.

Having a fight with someone you love is a great example of how this works. There has been a disagreement or a hurtful event. The ego takes over to protect itself. It will use its best logic and verbal ability to manufacture the divide between the two parties and help us argue the case of how we have been wronged. Better yet, it will help us argue how we are right and the other person is wrong. Whoever does this best feels superior. The verbal lashing that ensues can be messy and even more hurtful. Inevitably one or both parties becomes seduced by the overwhelming desire to win. They retreat to their corners.

At some point, the reconciliation begins. We recognize that fighting about what happened will keep us in the past. Slowly but surely, communicating about what we want moving forward will start to bring us back to our senses. When we find union again instead of separation, the feelings of love flood back even more intensely than before the fight began. It has now become more meaningful and satisfying to come together than to be apart.

Ironically, the process of calming the judging mind requires separation at first. To learn how to compartmentalize and keep the critical judgment away from our better thinking means pushing it aside. It may need to be locked away so it can do no harm until it is rehabilitated. Once we have learned the mental discipline of editing the judgment, we can then start to integrate our whole mind. We learn to accept the judger as a flip side to our personality that we can choose to disobey. We can allow it back in and know it is not the ultimate truth.

I have come a long way in calming my judgmental mind, although it can snap back into championship form so very quickly if I let it. When I was the self-proclaimed fashion police of Manhattan as I mentioned, I believed I was superior. In truth, when I look back, this was during the most miserable, depressed time of my life. It goes to show how powerful the mind is to lull us into a false sense of safety—the ego's safety. The place where we are so isolated and separate from others that the ego can own us and we don't even realize we are missing. The ego wants to keep us away from connection, compassion, unity, and the discovery of true meaning. That's how it can survive. It's like the dysfunctional relationship where one partner is controlling whom the other talks to and sees. The dominant one limits the other's contact with family in order to own the person completely, to assuage fears and insecurities that the partner might leave. The ego wants this level of power over us too, and the mind is its accomplice.

Upon my initiation, before my ordination, I had to write and declare my own vow of service. My personal vow of ministry is as follows:

"With deep gratitude and humility, I come before God, to pledge my being as a vehicle for service. I vow to see all beings as blessed expressions of God and to practice, live, and embrace loving-kindness with them and myself. I accept and dedicate myself to the continual growth this will require."

Keeping my own judgment at bay is part of my work. Whether I am coaching people or sitting with them in a ministry context, I am invited into their most personal thoughts and feelings. It is a privilege and honor to be there, and to earn it I have to remain neutral and unattached. I am not supposed to take sides. The secrets, weak spots, and fears I hold for these people must be locked away in a vault inside my brain, not to be brought up unless it is in service to them. If I interact with someone outside a coaching session, those precious secrets never come out of the vault. I am to know that person as he wants to be known in his public persona. Otherwise, those treasures could become weapons.

Truthfully, it is easier to do this in my work than in contexts where my consciousness is not as focused or raised as high. I had a humbling lesson about this a couple of years ago in a conversation with a childhood friend. Past history had preserved our friendship, but geographical distance kept us from being well connected. We also operate on different belief systems and found it hard to talk about personal things, which contributed to our infrequent contact. In an attempt to strengthen our relationship, I thought hitting on some points that we'd avoided before might be beneficial to us both. I was very, very wrong.

My friend and I had both been given opportunities for education that not all in our extended families had enjoyed. I always wondered why my friend, once on the path to taking premed courses, chose not to pursue any particular career path and instead had worked in administrative jobs for almost two decades. I asked in hopes of understanding her better and bridging a better connection, but instead I stepped on a land mine.

"Who are you to judge my choice of work?" she

exploded. "It was good enough for both of our mothers, why isn't it good enough for me?"

Wow. I hadn't realized that I had judged her. I knew how brilliantly smart she was and how underused she felt in each of her administrative jobs. I thought I was simply wanting more for her, but I had to admit that I had passed judgment. It was subtle, but it was so. I had been looking down on her for not doing more with what I felt she had. I was humbled by that and shifted immediately to knowing that the only way to move the relationship forward was to accept her for exactly who she is, no more, no less.

From there, I hoped we'd have a chance at a more meaningful relationship.

We've all been judged in one form or another. Whether it was by a parent, a teacher, a boss, or a friend, we know what it feels like to be judged. Some of us may have even had the misfortune of being falsely accused of a big infraction. And still, with the mental and physical memory of that pain, we can't help doing it to others and, often, to ourselves.

One of my pet peeves in the social realm occurs when someone has been trusted with my private world and I have to endure a ribbing at my own expense in front of others. If I've shared things with someone that are later used publicly to one-up me or embarrass me, I have to question what that person's motivation is. When I ask, a common response from people is: "I was just kidding!"

Let's look at the motivation for "just kidding." Who gets to be "up" and who gets to be "down" when we slap people publicly with a joke at their expense? You may have thought you were just kidding, but your ego was trying to be superior or gain power and your undisciplined mind allowed it. There's a time and a place for humor with friends, and I can zing a joke with the best of them, but when comedy becomes another form of condemnation, we have to see through the disguise to our desire for power—and thus separation—the root of feeling that meaning is missing.

Clearly, the need for growth continues. It is a constant exercise in mindfulness and compassion to find greater meaning to the little dramas of life that want to smack us back into knee-jerk reactions. It takes time and patience with ourselves and others to climb over the obstacles that the mind and the ego wants to put in the way of harmony with the people around us. It's so much easier to stop at the base of the mountain of judgment and only see the limited view. It takes great effort to climb to the top and see more clearly for miles and miles around. The view from there is inspiring. It's the feeling we all want for our lives of unlimited possibilities and a connection to the beauty of the natural order of things. That view is attainable whether we are looking in the mirror or into the face of another person. When we realize we are they and they are we, that in essence we are one, judgment would be impossible without condemning ourselves as well. When we clear our minds from the judgment of others and ourselves and even situations, we are free. Meaning shifts from being a sense of superiority to a sense of oneness and connection.

PART FIVE

MYSTIC

To be a mystic is to have direct access to the divine, an access that requires no middleman or woman. Mysticism is to have direct knowledge through insight and intuition of God or ultimate truth. In this state of overwhelming awe and connection to all things, meaning and purpose are a given. And here's what is truly surprising: the whole "mystic" thing is actually not as mysterious as it's been cracked up to be.

The Buddha, the "Awakened One," said that Buddha nature is in each one of us and that nothing special is required to have it. It's just a matter of allowing it. It is the same for the mystic in each one of us. Though the part of each of us that is capable of a higher consciousness and therefore connection to all things may be dormant, it is always accessible. Search your mind and heart for it, and it is there. And once awakened, the ultimate clarity and meaning result.

Within every spiritual tradition, the highest human ideal has always been some form of enlightenment. Whether it be accepting Jesus as savior or living Jewish law to the letter, most all religious doctrines lay out a structure for the achievement of pureness and goodness. To reach that highest ideal, however, it seems that we cannot escape pushing the limits on what is socially acceptable behavior. The Buddha sat under a tree for forty days, after years of searching preceded by his leaving his family and his envied royal position. Jesus was so bizarre to those with power that he became worthy of crucifixion. Some modern mystics have explored states of consciousness by using psychedelic drugs. Practitioners of the Mevlevi order of Sufism, known to some as "whirling dervishes," reach an altered state by spinning around and around. Saint Paul preached that a true Christian must "become a fool that he may become wise." All this to say that often the greatest joy, peace, and enlightenment will come from less than "proper" behavior. It is often from the place where not everyone is willing to go to that we can see life for all it is. The question becomes, How do we walk the line of worldly sanity and mysticism? Can we?

Mysticism and exaggeration go together. A mystic must not fear ridicule if he is to push all the way to the limits of humility or the limits of delight.

—Milan Kundera

~ ~ ~

Energy of the Universe, ground me in all that is not worldly so I may understand this world. Help me embrace the vision that allows pure freedom of heart and mind. Guide me to live from the power of knowing and the humility of sharing. I invite ultimate knowledge and infinite joy. Give me the strength to handle these gifts so I may grow and use them for good.

~ ~ ~

FIFTEEN

Dual Citizenship

A lot of us are like bad rental tenants. We think because "the place" isn't ours we don't have to be as careful with it or care about its contents the way we would our own. As I've said elsewhere in this book, we can behave similarly in our attitudes toward the environment, our bodies, and often our relationships. We need to understand that we are not just inhabitants of this planet but rather citizens.

The mystic's aim is to be not only *in* the world, but also *of* the world. She transcends the five senses to inhabit the wide world of the sixth sense, commonly called intuition. But more than just intuition is involved—there is a deep and enduring awareness that we are intrinsically connected to all things. Here, we float in a suspended reality that can at first feel foreign, but then becomes our operating system for a meaningful way of life.

Most of us have our worldly selves and our spiritual selves, and never the two shall meet. We mostly inhabit our worldly selves, pausing only to become our spiritual selves during our "day of worship" or our "morning meditation." Today's world, however, demands what I call Dual Citizenship—where we integrate both selves all the time. When we honor the spiritual in the worldliest of situations, we make more conscious and informed decisions that are not only for our personal benefit, but are also for the highest good of all concerned. When we live with an understanding and certainty about our essence, we can ease our worldly lives. When we stop acting from fear and start behaving from the side of ourselves that is wise, we make a better world for everyone. And if you are still wondering where to find meaning, this integration beckons.

My time in Alaska with Mark was messy and emotional, and it was also when the integration began for me. I thought I had a handle on the deep depression that had been plaguing me, but I was still having frequent setbacks. One of the most dramatic was getting news that a friend's mother had a relapse of cancer. Radiation treatment had halted a thyroid cancer that had claimed her once healthy jaw, teeth, and salivary glands. We thought she was out of the woods. Then another mass was found in her breast. My friend's mother had become a mentor of mine over the years. This news had hit me particularly hard.

By this time, I had been a student of A Course in Miracles for a few years, and it was bringing me peace and helping me heal. However, as I sat in my dorm room at the Alaska resort's crew camp and read the letter with this bad news, I threw the course book, my bible at the time, across the room and against the wall several times. I howled deep, agonizing cries. After a few more throws of the book, I felt as if I were watching myself from outside my body. I almost could not believe I was behaving that way, but the recognition of it let me engage in it deeper. Fear was taking root as well because I had the presence of mind to know that the grief was returning and the depression was not over. I cried for my mentor, for myself, and for every unfair thing I could think of.

In a tears-induced stupor, I took myself outside, several hundred feet from the crew camp on a lone tall rock. My rock and I were in an open field facing Mount Healy, where the Alaska Railroad train connects Fairbanks to Seward and often passes right in front of me. On top of this rock, overlooking this vast plateau, I howled and screamed and cried until there was no emotion left. In my rawness, I was without thought or feeling of any kind. Then I started to feel everything. I could reach the distant mountains across the river from me. I could feel them in my heart. I was so connected to the sky that I felt enveloped by its dim gray-and-orange hue. I could feel the tall, wheatlike grass surrounding my single rock perch. I did not see any wildlife, but I could feel them: bears, caribou, birds, and arctic squirrels. I had transcended the emotion and fear and was in a mystical space. I was okay. I did not know my mentor's fate, but I was back in a hopeful connected place where the world was friendly and I was no longer alone. I was moving with the flow of energetic fields in the world instead of pushing against them with my own agenda. If that is God or that is Divine, then I was there in the God-space.

My mentor dealt with her illness in her own private way, keeping contact with other people to a minimum. I sent cards and left messages for her, knowing she might never want to speak to me directly. Still, I felt that I was there with her, even though I was thousands of miles away. (She made it, and is alive and well today.)

After the big cry on the rock, I knew something had shifted in me and, as the days and weeks went on, the confirmation of this I received was very unusual. Suddenly, children were reacting to me in a unique way. Until this point in my life, I was not particularly fond of children, and I had already told Mark that to marry me meant a life with no kids. I had no interest in them, and they kept their distance from me. The first glimpse that this had changed came one night while I was singing my big solo in the hotel's dinner show where we worked. It's important to say that the show Mark and I were doing was not something we *ever* intended to put on our professional acting résumés. Quality it was not. We took the job as a paid way to see Alaska. On alternate nights, I played the dinner hall hostess dressed like a can-can girl or the proprietor of a Yukon saloon, a tomboy in work boots, jeans, and a man's flannel hunting shirt. On this particular night as the proprietor, it was time to sing my big ballad. I can't remember what is was called, but I know it was a contemplative song about something Alaskan. As I wandered away from the small stage and onto the dance floor and then over to the big picture window that looked out to pines and Alaskan views, toddlers and young kids followed me. One by one they left their parents' side at the log mess-hall tables and came to join me at the big window. By the time I noticed, there must have been fifteen little people around me. I started getting choked up as I sang; I knew what was happening.

Something had shifted. I wasn't scary to kids anymore. I had walked through some kind of portal, which it would still take some years for me to fully recognize and name.

I was not a sole inhabitant anymore with my unique brand of problems, I was a citizen and aware of a new connection. That connection was not a burden but rather a coveted invitation to embrace life more fully and in a more meaningful way. To keep this awareness in our modern, fast world is tough, but it is possible through dedicated practice. Once I had touched it, I knew I wanted more.

Almost every religious tradition has its mystic counterpart. Judaism has Kabbalah, Islam has Sufism, and Christianity has its desert mystics—its mothers and fathers and Gnostics. Sidestepping most religions that make it necessary to have a religious leader or servant of God in order to connect with a divine presence, many mystic traditions encourage people to strike that connection themselves. In a time where organized religion is still very popular but may be losing its grip on society as the ultimate provider of truth, people are grappling with finding meaning for themselves. By going back to the ancient belief that we all have direct access to the collective consciousness often called God, many modern people can create that meaning for themselves without a "middleman" or house of worship to do so. We don't need a doctrine or predetermined path to get there.

In religions and houses of worship, we commune with one another and God. We come together, we join for a period of time, and we learn from that connection. It feels meaningful to a lot of us. What mysticism provides is the opportunity to go beyond communion to union. To reach a sustainable state of direct knowledge and assimilation versus a temporary visit whose benefit fades. Granted, by definition, the majority of mystical experiences last only a short time, but the knowledge and insight that are gained become assimilated and permanent. Communing is limited to a time and a place, while union is without borders. To gather together to learn, study, sing, and worship is fine and feeds the human spirit. It can, however, keep us split between our worldly selves and our spiritual selves, if we let it. Our evolution requires more. To sustain meaning and have it integrated into our lives means nurturing union at all times. There, we lose all sense of self and subject-object duality, which results in feeling and being connected to all things.

An early Islamic scholar, Al-Ghazali, who became a Sufi, a Muslim mystic, said: "I turned to the way of the mystics. . . . [I] obtained a thorough understanding of their principles. Then I realized that what is most distinctive of them can only be obtained by personal experience [taste], ecstasy and change of character. . . . I saw clearly that the mystics were men of personal experience not of words, that I had gone as far as possible by way of study and intellectual application, so only personal experience and walking in the mystic way were left."[1]

Jesus was a mystic—walking sure, grounded, and knowing his connection to his source, his God. A religion was created around him. The Buddha, Lao Tzu, Mohammed, and all the great teachers who walked the earth set a mark for the mere mortal to reach in getting closer to enlightenment. Their followers cemented a religion around their teaching; the teachers themselves did not. That is, the mystics came first and the institutionalization of their ideas followed. Something got lost in the translation, but there would be no way to preserve the wisdom if it had not been "packaged" for consumption. Huston Smith said: "If you do not institutionalize your spirituality, it gets no traction on history. So if Jesus had not been followed by Saint Paul, who established a

---

[1]Quoted in W. Montgomery Watt, *Muslim Intellectual: A Study of Al-Ghazali* (Edinburgh: Edinburgh University Press, 1963).

church, the Sermon on the Mount would have evaporated within a generation. . . . We have to understand the burdens of institutionalization—and they are heavy."[2] Religions and their ancient texts were products of the cultures in which they were conceived. The call now is to understand those limits and use them to connect, to become Dual Citizens. To be integrated is to draw from all that is available.

All people have the potential to attain the same state of consciousness demonstrated by Jesus and the other great teachers. We can all be mystics and you certainly don't have to believe in God, a supreme being, to do so. We just have to open to the source of all that is, regardless of what we call it—science, nature, cosmos, or nothing. The important thing is that it centers our existence. We understand, however, it is fine because with each step of acceptance and ease in our beliefs, more will be revealed to bring comfort and understanding.

Elie Wiesel asks the question: "What does mysticism really mean?" His answer? "It means the way to attain knowledge. It's close to philosophy, except in philosophy you go horizontally while in mysticism you go vertically."

[2]Quoted in John Horgan, *Rational Mysticism* (New York: Houghton Mifflin, 2003).

What I think he meant is that in philosophy we still apply logic to our explanations of how the world works, creating a linear, horizontal plane of understanding. Mysticism claims no such logic, but certainly, deeper-rooted (vertical) conviction of Truth. It is said that the eternal Truth is God, but it transcends that. The mind and ego are highly engaged if they are dealing with God as the higher being. Beyond God is the connection with all being. That is where we need to invite ourselves to go. It's even more inclusive. It's even more universally fair. There is no interpretation needed. It just is. There is no argument about which God or how to get there or even if it is God. It is the greatest expanse of being and it's readily available to us right now.

Applying this to our worldly existence takes effort. As a mystic in business in the five-sensory world, I have made some unpopular decisions. I remember one when I was barely thirty and I was in a meeting of about a dozen professionals gathered to hear about a business opportunity that could benefit us all. The profession was young, and any chance at an opportunity to bring coaching into a corporation was a milestone and a very desirable and profitable possibility.

We were in a hotel conference room, taking some time

away from a business symposium we were all attending, and the air was formal as I took my seat at the table. We were each in our comfortable, executive-type chairs with notebooks in front of us, and the man with the opportunity to share was at the head of the table. I was the youngest of the bunch, which was par for the course for me. Our host was just about to begin to present his treasure, when I spoke suddenly, surprising even myself.

"This is awkward, but I am going to excuse myself from this conversation," I said.

I started packing up my belongings, trying to exit quickly as to not take too much focus off the meeting.

"Why don't you tell us what's on your mind," the host said.

I had half expected him to ask, and half hoped that I would get out of there without having to explain, because I wasn't even sure why I was leaving. This was an elite group of folks; anyone would have killed to be invited into this circle. But I knew I had to leave.

It was not a logical thought process. I felt I was floating in an altered reality, without control over my mouth and the thoughts that became words through it. I felt like I was channeling someone else, but it was me acting on pure instinct and feeling very guided to do so.

Amid minor protests and perfunctory good-byes, I left. In my body I could feel the "rightness" of the move, but I could not reconcile it in my mind. I did not let myself get stressed over it. I knew I had walked away from an enviable opportunity, but I knew on a much deeper level that I did not belong there, although I had no reason or logical explanation. Within two months, I had clarity as to the wisdom of that unusual move. Without much warning or dedicated effort on my part, I was catapulted into a national level of media exposure and on my way to deciding between two publishers who wanted rights to a first book. The gentle hand of something beyond my reasoning left brain had pulled me away from one thing to be available to something else entirely.

That was a mystical experience. It was circumventing logic and the tested ways of succeeding. It was not five-sensory. It was beyond logic and linear time or effort. I felt connected to guidance that I could not even explain. I had a knowing beyond reason.

A fear still exists that opening up to a connection greater than what our religious upbringing professes to give us, we are making ourselves vulnerable to ridicule or even worse, dark forces and the occult. Practicing dark magic, performing rituals, ingesting hallucinogenic aides, or being part of an ancient indigenous ceremony are certainly tried-and-true routes for some, but they are not a prerequisite for a mystic. Sure, there are people who say that is a playground they prefer, but it is not necessary to have séances or eat mushrooms to connect with a spirit or have a universal sense of connection.

There was a time when I thought that being a mystic meant having spiritual guides. I have known people who claim they have spirit guides and angels that send guidance and teams of helpers from the beyond. I don't think they are crazy. I respect their reality, and often I felt I'd be more spiritually enlightened if I had such other-worldly ammunition. Someone in my own circle who is a mystic told me to ask for my guides to make themselves known to me. I was determined to have a support team, so I did.

Before bed one night, I asked fervently in prayer for my guides to make themselves known. I fell asleep as usual, but at some point in the night I rolled over and heard my name being called. When I turned to the side of my bed near my dresser, I saw a small crowd of children waving at me. They were my guides. I was so freaked by this episode that I let out an involuntary yelp and asked them to go away. I've never called on them again.

I feel guided, protected, and led in other ways, but have not felt the need to have guides again. I don't feel any less spiritual for it. My point is that the connection to meaning I am speaking of is available without becoming a medium or psychic advisor (although nothing is wrong with that!). I have psychic periods of very heightened intuition and I use intuition in my work.

There are other experiences that lead me to believe there is more to our Dual Citizenship existence beyond what we have logical explanation for. For example, when I was pregnant with my twins, I went to see a trusted psychic advisor. I went to her because she is always accurate in her readings and surprises me with her ability to see what I am not yet aware of or privy to. On this particular day, she asked me what I was going to name my baby girl, who then was the only baby I was aware of. (I found out I was carrying twins at eighteen weeks.) I knew intuitively that it was a girl. I had not had medical confirmation. I said that we were naming her Maya Rose. After welling up with the love that saying her name out loud gave me, I smelled flowers in the air. I asked my friend if she smelled them and she said no. I got up from my chair and smelled every bowl and candle in her small studio, trying to find the source of the floral scent. There was no physical evidence.

I'm sure science could say that I had some kind of sense memory upon saying "Rose," but I felt convinced that my baby girl's way to me was confirmed. To me it meant as much as her waving to me from a sonogram. She let me know she was there.

Is that crazy? Is it scientifically provable? Is it mystical? Is it spiritual? It was meaningful to me and came from beyond logical, linear thinking. As I've defined mysticism here, it was mystical.

I have always felt that if I tell the truth about something, it may give another person the courage to do the same or offer a feeling of not being alone. I know of many closeted "woo-woos," mystics, and members of the Dual Citizenship club—people who feel that they would be ridiculed if they spoke of the stranger experiences they have had when they open themselves to what is beyond our five-sensory, safe existence. We cannot be a mystic from there. To connect to the meaning we crave, we are required to tap our sixth sense to access inner knowledge and the union with divine nature. That union is equal to freedom. It is beyond space and time and often beyond language. Dionysius the Areopagite, a mysterious fifth-to-sixth-century monk, once said of the mystical path: "The more it climbs, the more language falters, and when it has passed up and beyond the ascent, it will turn silent completely, since it will finally be at one with [that] which is indescribable."

The Dual Citizen is not afraid of the soul, even when the mind cannot understand what is happening. The soul predates you, and the wisdom you possess is its memory. Letting our inner life lead our life, when it is not based in fear, is the hope of the times.

SIXTEEN

A New Spirituality Emerging

On a recent flight, I was sitting next to a mom and child who were separated from the other half of their family by a row and an aisle. There was no way to get them together, so I was part of helping them as the unavoidable struggles came up. I was busier than I would have liked, but I really didn't mind. The woman directly across the aisle from me was a good distraction whenever I needed a break from being the surrogate nanny.

The woman across the aisle had exotic looks: long, dark, curly hair; deep, dark eyes; and brown skin. Her jewelry had a Gypsy-like flair. She saw that I had a *mala* (string of Buddhist prayer beads) wrapped around my wrist, and asked me what it was. She compared the *mala* to the equivalent in her Islamic tradition. She asked if I was Buddhist. I had told her I was not a Buddhist per se and that I was raised Jewish. She told me she was Pakistani and had been living in America for many years. She explained how important being a Muslim was for her and how much she loved her religion. I asked her why she didn't wear a head covering. She said that although she was almost sixty, she was too modern for such things, but that it did not mean she loved her religion any less. We talked freely and asked each other questions about each other's culture and faith. She abruptly stopped and asked:

"How come you know so much about my faith and some of these others?"

I told her that a year before, I had graduated from a seminary whose focus it was to expose me to many religious traditions.

Pointing her finger at me and scrunching her face with a passionate intensity, she said in her accent: "More people should be like you. The world would be better off!"

The hair on my arms stood on end. For a moment, we "pinged" like a set of Tibetan prayer cymbals (*tingsha*), and it felt to me as if our combined energies sent a ripple of love out to the ether. There was a moment of "oneness" that felt delicious and mystical. We had bypassed any need to remain distinct or special, to find a universal connection.

I would call this kind of connection an instance of Modern Mysticism. In the above case, the connection to the divine had come from a connection between two human beings. At another time, it might be a connection in nature, or space or timelessness or some other aspect of our existence. But this time it was two humans connecting at least two cultures and the long histories that come with them. And this Modern Mysticism as such is available to us all at any time.

The word *mystic* derives from the Greek *mystes*, the term for an initiate. *Mystikos*, which is related to this term, means "seeing with eyes closed." These definitions suggest that we do indeed need to close our eyes and shut out the data of our five senses, or at least give them a rest in order to connect with our sixth sense. There, we enter the mystery of divine nature, not knowing, infinite possibilities, and all that is. As we become more conscious, our human bandwidth expands to handle mysticism. In our continued search for meaning as a species, a new spirituality is emerging and mysticism is very much a part of it.

Ken Wilber, modern-day philosopher, says that mystical awareness is simply the culmination of cognitive development. Once we have exercised our intellectual capacities, we begin to long for more and to respond to the call to not just think about the world differently, but to also change ourselves, the thinkers. And it is this critical change in perception that allows for more connection and meaning.

Earlier I mentioned how the recovery from my deepest depression involved digging to find a sprig of gratitude that would enable me to turn my thinking from despair to a hint of lightness. I had to see and think about things differently. I had to stop deciding that I knew what everything was. In other words, I had to question whether my perception of things, even something as common as a spoon, was to be depended on. Clearly, a spoon is a spoon—for eating or for scooping—but to change the thinker, I had to leave the spoon open to interpretation. That's how the healing of my suffering mind began. The judgment and certainty of my belief system had caused attachment and pain. Without judgment as a force, I was a curious learner willing to be open to a new experience. And without judgment, I did not hurt.

Back in the white loft, the thinker had begun to transform. When I could feel the connection to the people that would be coming there for help, there were hints of mysticism in the white space. The thinking and then the feelings shifted from pain to connection. From singular and individual to global. Simultaneously, I could find meaning in the pain and extend that realization into purposeful action. I was energized and moved in a way that did not seem physically possible only moments before.

For months after, to keep the change going, I paid so much attention to my thoughts that I'd feel a sickness at times akin to reading in a car. I was so tired—often I had to sleep during the day to have the strength and energy to push through such a mental exercise. At the time, I thought of it as constantly having to change the tapes in my head. I censored every thought. I had to be sure I was allowing to cement only those that would work in my favor versus against me. When my thoughts would attack me, my own voice filling my head telling me how useless and utterly pathetic I was, I had to stop the progression of thoughts that would follow and turn the whole internal conversation to a new direction. I'd think: "You can stop hurting yourself now. You are worth being kind to." I needed this level of mental attention to function in the most practical of ways, but over many years, the practice eventually gave way to a mystical awareness that felt meaningful. When I could stop the destruction inside my own head, I could begin to extend kindness outside myself as well. There was more room for other people and giving of myself and contributing. It was no longer a solitary existence but one that rang with joy. I felt the exaltation of one who is rejoining the world.

The emerging new spirituality is a desire to get rid of pretense and be real. Be real in our questions, in our doubts, in our convictions, and in our passions and pain. To have meaning we need things to be tangible; we need to feel. However, that which is tangible may not necessarily be in material form. "Real" will be a feeling, and it will be tangible in our mystical awareness and consciousness. It will resonate in our bodies and bring us to our senses, and cause us to be present and pay attention. We are being asked to raise our consciousness to feel the trust we need to move our lives forward with or without the aid of the institutions we have relied on in the past.

The current angst is a response to the call to grow and evolve. This existential pang repeats itself throughout history and cultures. But what seems to be new is that we are evolving at a faster rate without time to integrate the change before the next thing is asked of us. We have been thrown into a large wave of evolutionary growth without swimming lessons or lifesaving devices. We are trying to row in the same vessel on the same course we always have, but that won't work.

It's fair to say that in the past, we have looked to religion to fill this need. The ultimate point of following any religion and its path is to reach enlightenment (an ultimate existence), which we can equate to many definitions of mystical awareness. Whether it's salvation through Jesus' love and then entrance to heaven, or enlightenment in the Buddhist sense reached through meditation, or Islamic enlightenment through devotion, every tradition holds out for the ultimate union of body, mind, and spirit. Yet I dare suggest that the next step, the emerging spirituality, is the yearning to be mystics. It is a truth greater than any because we experience it ourselves. We do not have to rely on anyone or any institution to provide the path to it. Meaning waits in the moment of experience—not in the telling, the retelling, the writing down, or the rehashing. It comes in the experience and the moment. For only now can you be in the experience. You can't really relate it or re-create it exactly as it was. It just is. The new spirituality is an infinity of "nows" strung together and suspended from the columns that hold up our life.

Being full of love, peace, hope, compassion, patience, and appreciation for everything and connection to all things. These feelings make up meaning. These feelings change our physiology—they can alter cells. They can transform water, as was described by Masaru Emoto.[2] These have come about through religion and ritual, but they don't have to. They can be the currency of every day if we really want them to.

If life feels meaningless, we have to hold back from the impulse to snuff it out. Instead, we need to seek *more* of it free of interpretations, expectations, and separation. To seek out more life means seeking out living things— people and nature—all that can grow. Seek out connection with what lives and breathes and watch the pieces come together. If life feels meaningless it is because we forgot who we are and that we have a purpose to fulfill— to live a life that works with reverence, awe, and love present at its core. What is emerging is the possibility that we are finally ready to put this into action and that this might truly be the answer after all, even if we have ignored that message in religions for thousands of years.

It is the modern mystic who will lead the way. What's possible is that in remembering who we really are and

[2]Masaru Emoto, the author of *The Message from Water*, is known for his controversial claim that if human thoughts are directed at water before it freezes, the resulting images in ice will reflect whether the thoughts were positive or negative.

living in a more conscious space, we can stand fully in the understanding that what we do affects everyone and everything. It is only with that conscious awareness of our interconnectedness that the world we all hope for can result. Just as the global economy now makes it impossible for any one country to really hope for the demise of another because it would mean deep troubles for itself, so are we being called to unify in our beliefs to bring our world back into balance. A global economy includes all forms of currency (dollar, euro, peso, and so on) but has to operate as one. Our role as mystics is to allow the variations in belief, but elevate our consciousness to one universal, magnificent truth about our essential being.

> A religion old or new, that stressed the magnificence of the universe as revealed by modern science, might be able to draw forth reserves of reverence and awe hardly tapped by the conventional faiths. Sooner or later, such a religion will emerge.
>
> —Dr. Carl Sagan

The modern mystic is integrated—the worldly self and the spiritual self working as one. The modern mystic is you.

Collective Consciousness, the power that holds us all, may we feel your presence, and, as a result, feel our own. May we root deeply into our own being and be present to all of our human emotions and our everlasting soul. May the integration of ourselves be the key to our connection to all things. May we recognize the power we are and the power we have to straighten the crooked places in our world. May we recognize the possibility for goodness in all things and live fully in that consciousness. May we recognize this as a meaningful life.

And so it is.

ACKNOWLEDGMENTS

This book was conceived on the day after I graduated from interfaith seminary, so it's only fitting to start
by thanking the extraordinary class of 2006, who were
some of the greatest teachers I've ever had. And to the
staff and directors at One Spirit Learning Alliance and
One Spirit Interfaith Seminary, thank you for the great
work you do and the important courses you offer. Special
thanks to the director, the Reverend Diane Berke, for
your friendship and mentorship.

David Hale Smith of DHS Literary, thank you for
being there for me as I stumbled through the ways in
which I wanted to express myself in book form. Your
patience, expertise, and friendship really made the difference. A shout-out to Shauyi Tai for your kindness.

Thank you to Linda Siversten for your support with the proposal for this book. Your influence is on these pages.

My publisher, Joel Fotinos, is a good friend and a firm believer in all things LBF. What a unique and rare gift to have this kind of relationship. I can't thank you enough for holding a vision for me of what I could do as a writer and waiting for me to grow into it. Sara Carder, my editor, keeps me from making a fool of myself and was instrumental in making this book work. Thank you, Sara, for your craftsmanship, care, and friendship. Katherine Obertance, Brianna Yamashita, Tara Dosh, Kelli Daniel-Richards, the sales team, and all the other folks at Tarcher who made this happen: thank you so much. Thanks also to the copy editor, Diane Hodges.

This book would not have been written (at least not on time) without my very dear friend the talented writer Jennifer Louden, whom I met after she endorsed *Living Your Best Life*. She gave it such a glowing review that I had to call her to thank her, and we've been friends ever since. Thank you for coaching me and keeping me on track, and for your honesty, tenderness, and interest. And all those cuts—God, they were hard to take, but you were right.

Without my assistant, Christina Janscik, I'd have no life and no business. You allow me room to breathe and keep me on track. Thank you for your hard work, your companionship, and most of all your enthusiasm for what I do. I hope your dreams come true. Thank you as well to the team of talented coaches at Now What?® Coaching: Cassi Christiansen, Jeanne McLennan, Deborah Roth, Nancy Friedberg, and Grace Durfee. Talented professionals who are successful in your own right, you all take time to support my efforts, and I appreciate our relationship and our work together. A shout-out to all the coaches who are authorized Now What?® facilitators and all those I know through the International Coach Federation and Coach University who have been cheerleaders and supporters for years. Bobette Reeder, Donna Steinhorn, Guy Stickney, Sandy Vilas, Margaret Krigbaum, thank you with sugar on top.

There are so many friends and family to thank. If I have left anyone out, please forgive me. Donna Ellis, Carolynn Turkalo, Lysa Dahlin, DJ Mitsch, Madeleine Homan, thank you for the history of long friendships and the consistency of your love. I am eternally grateful. To neighbors Michelle and Ken Posner, Shelly White, Laura Harrington, Megan Lavoie, Amy and Terri Pender, Laura Morowitz and Eric Schecter, thank you for saving my butt, picking up my kids, feeding us great meals, and just being good folks who make life easier and more fun.

You are amazing, generous people. In-laws Grandma Joan and Captain Morty, what would I do without you? Thank you, Amy and Gene Connor. And to my mom and dad, Fran and Bert Berman, I am so glad my kids get to enjoy you, and I am so grateful for your help. I can't do this life without all of you.

To my husband, Mark, I owe a debt of gratitude; I know you are there, always believing in me more than I believe in myself. Thanks for ping-ponging child care with me and trying to make life easier for me. We are partners in the dance of life, and we ain't finished yet. We have those amazing kids, Skyler, Maya, and Wyatt. You three have taught me how to write in less and less time as you've needed me more—that's a good thing! I love you. You are what keeps me real and wanting to flourish. Thanks for letting Mommy write and go away every now and then. It makes me feel good to contribute in the world, and I think it makes me a better mom too. Thank you, my yummy family, for your support and for being there. Coming home to you is what makes it all worthwhile.

http://www.thelittlebookonmeaning.com
Free quiz. Free audio podcasts. See the movie. Download
an extra chapter. Read the blog "A Meaningful Life."

Laura Berman Fortgang
c/o Now What?® Coaching
26 Park Street, Suite 2045
Montclair, NJ 07044
(973) 857-8180
www.nowwhatcoaching.com
www.laurabermanfortgang.com

One Spirit Learning Alliance
330 West 38th Street, Suite 1500
New York, NY 10018
(212) 931-6840
www.onespiritinterfaith.org
Training programs include the One Spirit Interfaith
Seminary, the One Spirit Conscious Leadership Institute, and the Interspiritual Counseling Program. There
are also shorter courses and programs open to the public
on a wide range of topics related to personal and spiritual
development.

LAURA BERMAN FORTGANG is the author of *Now What? 90 Days to a New Life Direction*, *Living Your Best Life*, and the national bestseller *Take Yourself to the Top*. Known as a pioneer in the personal coaching field, she is the founder of Now What?® Coaching and a cofounder of the International Coach Federation. As a professional speaker, she has traveled to many parts of the world in an effort to raise consciousness and inspire excellence for individuals, companies, and seekers of all kinds. Fortgang is an ordained interfaith minister and lives with her husband and their three children in Montclair, New Jersey.

Other Laura Berman Fortgang titles
available from Tarcher

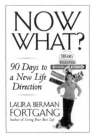

Now What?
90 Days to a New Life Direction

978-1-58542-413-9

Living Your Best Life:
Discover Your Life's Blueprint for Success

978-1-58542-157-2

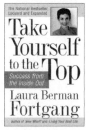

Take Yourself to the Top:
Success from the Inside Out

978-1-58542-447-4